THE

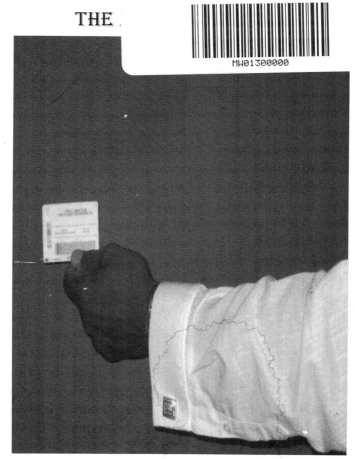

WHO AM I?

LEE B. CUMMINGS

(THE NEGRO QUESTION)

Copyright © 2011 by (LEE BERNARD CUMMINGS)

TXU001774531

All rights reserved. No part of this book may be reproduced or transmitted

in any form or by any means without written permission from the author.

ISBN# 1468181920

Dedication

I would like to give special honor to the Living God, for the gift of life that he has given to the angels, man and beast. I want to give a special thanks to my deceased parents, John and Verda Cummings. I'd like to give recognition to John, Norman, Lois, Eugene, Chris, Dr. Wan, my sons and daughter. I would like to say thanks, to all the elders who laid their lives down, for the benefits that the Negro in this generation enjoys.

Table of Contents

Chapter 1 BLACK BUT NOT AFRICAN THE BLACKS OF MESOPOTAMIA 5

Chapter 2 ISRAELITE COLONIES 19

Chapter 3 ISRAEL IN AFRICA 23

Chapter 4 THE SHIPS OF BABEL 47

Chapter 5 THE NEGRO RESISTANCE 58

Chapter 6 THE QUARREL OF THE COVENANT . 73

Chapter 7 IF IT BE A SON KILL HIM 89

Chapter 8 THE UNTHINKABLE 98

Chapter 9 THE MORNING TRAIN 105

Chapter 10 WAR WITH THE GOD OF ISRAEL .. 116

Chapter 11 THE ANSWER TO THE NEGRO QUESTION 127

Chapter 12 THE WHITE JEWISH QUESTION 130

Chapter 13 THE EUROPEAN SECRET 150

CONCLUSION 165

BIBLIOGRAPHY & REFERENCES 167

CHAPTER 1   BLACK   BUT   NOT   AFRICAN

Ever since the so called Negro came into contact with the European's through the slave trade, there have been a number of legitimate questions concerning this Negro. Number (1) which of the son's of Noah is his father? Number (2) where did the Negro have his origination? Number (3) is he African or Mesopotamian? Number (4) who is the Negro in America? In order to understand who the Negro is we must first begin this book with examining this picture found in Amari, (northwest Sumer) the brown skinned people in the picture are the ancient Sumerians (Mesopotamians) to the far right of the picture is a black African. Even though the Mesopotamian and African are black, they are different people. The Mesopotamians were black people and this is where Abraham had his origination in Ur (Sumer or Shinar).

Abraham the Mesopotamian was a black man and so were his descendants. This bust you are looking at is of Sargon the Great. Sargon's testimony was, "that **he ruled over the black headed people**". In the Tablets of Sumer, the people of Sumer describe themselves as the **black headed people**! This Sargon is a black Mesopotamia not Libyan (ancient name of Africa) and although **he is black he is not African!** The next image you should be looking at is an image of one of Shems' sons Elam, the Elamite, from the 10th chapter of Genesis and the 22nd verse it mentions Shems son, Elam. These Elamites were from

ELAMITE WARRIORS   **MODERN IRAQI**

KING SHULGI   **KING GUDEA**   **SARGON**

Mesopotamia and were clearly black people but they were not the sons of Ham. The three black kings, King Shulgi of UR, King Gudea of Lagash and King Sargon of Accad, were all Mesopotamian Kings, yet neither of these three black kings are the sons of Africa (Ham). In fact, Sargon the Great's rule extended from Elam to the Mediterranean Sea.

The People of Mesopotamia, Iraq and Iran still retain their blackness. Here is a quote from one historian concerning the people of Mesopotamia, **"the people of Mesopotamia are dark people (black) but not Negro".** Well if these people weren't Negro what were they? The Zondervan **Pictorial bible dictionary (page 330) states that Ham is the progenitor of Mizraim, Cush, Put, and Canaan but not the Negro!** As you can see Mesopotamia, was inhabited by black somewhat baldheaded people. This fact is of extreme importance when weighed on a scale with the evidence that I shall present. And so Abraham, the black Mesopotamian leaves Ur of Sumer (SHINAR) and heads into the land of Canaan Genesis the 11th chapter verses 31 and 32. Subsequently, Abraham has a son by the name of Isaac who in turn has a son by the name of Jacob. Remember that Abraham is a black man from Mesopotamia and his sons look like him. Let's proceed to the life of Jacob it is written in 1st Chronicles that Jacob (name changed to Israel) had twelve sons named, Rueben, Simeon, Levi, Judah, Issachar, Zebulon, Dan, Joseph, Benjamin, Naphtali, Gad, and Asher. Below are images of ancient

Egyptians, including one with Nefertiti, the queen of Egypt and King Tut. Notice that the ancient Egyptians and the modern

QUEEN NEFETERI

BOY KING TUT

MODERN EGYPTIANS LOOK LIKE THE ARTIFACTS

Egyptians are still black. If you said they don't look like the Arabs in Egypt today you are correct the so called Arabs in Egypt invaded Egypt in 640A.D and have been there ever since. Therefore the Egyptian citizen in Egypt today is not the descendant of the ancient Egyptians.

In fact the name **Egypt means black**; so now lets' go to a funeral scene where Jacob Israel is dying. In Genesis 47:28-31 Jacob dies, then in Genesis 50:7 – 11 all of Jacobs 12 sons and the princes of Egypt go up to bury Jacob. Waiting in the wings are the Canaanites who for some odd reason think that everybody in the funeral procession is an Egyptian because they are all black!

NEFETERI   **ELAM**   **HAGAB**
HAM SEED   **SHEM SEED**   **SHEM SEED**

AS YOU CAN CLEARLY SEE THE SEED OF HAM AND THE SEED OF SHEM HAVE THE SAME BLACK SKIN BUT THEY HAVE DIFFERENT FATHERS! **HAM IS FROM AFRICA** AND **SHEM IS FROM MESOPOTAMIA.**

Even though the three black persons on page 10 look alike, they are not of the same lineage. Nefeteri is from Ham's seed, the Elamite warrior or Mesopotamian is from Shem's seed and the Judean archer Hagab is also of Shem's seed (the tribe of Judah) which the Israelites descend from. Remember Abraham, Isaac and Jacob is descended from Shem. Of importance, this Nefertiti would be considered a Negro by today's use of the word. Lastly, there is an image of Joseph the son of Jacob the Mesopotamian in Egyptian garb.

The inscription reads Joseph viceroy of Egypt (SHEM SEED) As you can see, based on the coins image, the Joseph of the Bible was black. See article on next page.

ARTICLE:

An Egyptian paper claims that archaeologists have discovered ancient Egyptian coins bearing the name and image of the Biblical Joseph.

The report in Al-Ahram boasts that the find backs up the Koran's claim that coins were used in Egypt during Joseph's period. Joseph, son of the Patriarch Jacob, died around 1450 B.C.E., according to Jewish sources. Excerpts from the Al-Ahram report, as translated by Mideast Media:"In an unprecedented find, a group of Egyptian researchers and archaeologists has discovered a cache of coins from the time of the Pharaohs. Its importance lies in the fact that it provides decisive scientific evidence disproving the claim by some historians that the ancient Egyptians were unfamiliar with coins and conducted their trade through barter.**"The researchers discovered the coins when they sifted through thousands of small archaeological artifacts stored in [the vaults of] the Museum of Egypt. [Initially] they took them for charms, but a thorough examination revealed that the coins bore the year in which they were minted and their value, or effigies of the pharaohs [who ruled] at the time of their minting. Some of the coins are from the time when Joseph lived in Egypt, and bear his name and portrait.** So far, it should be obvious to you that MESOPOTAMIANS were and still are people of color but let's see if Shem's seed down to the time of Moses is still being mistaken for the sons of Ham, an Egyptian. Let's look at Moses, the seed of Shem, and see if he was also mistaken for an Egyptian. There is an interesting story in Exodus about a man named Jethro who had 7 daughters and how one day when they went to water the livestock they were being pushed away and Moses helped them. When the women came home the old man Jethro asked them why were they home so early and they said an Egyptian helped us. The word Egypt means black and that man they were referring to was none other than Moses! See Exodus the 2nd chapter the 16th thru the 25th verse. Let's see if this problem of the seed of Shem being mistaken for an Egyptian persisted 2000 yrs later to the times of the Apostle Paul. Lets run down to acts and ear hustle (listen in on) on a conversation a Roman soldier is having with Paul. See Acts the 21st chapter the 37th thru the 40th verse. The Roman soldier asked Paul if he was that Egyptian who led 400 men into the wilderness but Paul's response was," I am a Jew. In Romans 11:1 he is specific and tells the reader that he is from the tribe of Benjamin! After 2000 yrs the seed of Shem, the Mesopotamian, which became Israel, is still being mistaken for Hams seed the African. **The ZONDERVAN PICTORIAL BIBLE DICTIONARY QUOTES" HAM IS THE**

FATHER OF MIZRAIM, CUSH, PHUT AND CANAAN BUT NOT THE NEGRO!! So if Ham is not the Negros father and Japheth is not the Negros father that leaves only one son of Noah and ladies and gentlemen that is Shem! He is the father of the Israelites. I shall proceed to show you how the black Mesopotamians or Hebrew Israelites made there way to the west coast of Africa. Any Pastor worth a hill of beans knows that there were 5 incidents that proceeded to push the black Israelites into the interior of Africa: (1) The ancient black Assyrians came up and invaded Israel in 722 b.c taking out the ten tribes (2) Nebuchadnezzar destroyed Jerusalem and carried away captive Benjamin, Judah, and Levi in 606 B.C and 587 B.C (3) The Romans sacked Jerusalem in 70 A.D, (4) The Arabs under the Caliphs invaded Jerusalem in 640 A.D and in 132 A.D when Hadrian Caesar destroyed Jerusalem and forbade the Jews from entering into the gates of the city. Every time Israel needed a place to escape from her enemies she proceeded into the heart of Libya (the ancient name of Africa). Is there any proof in the Bible to substantiate such a boastful claim? Let's turn to the book of Acts and see what the Holy Ghost had the Apostle Peter to tell the congregation where Israel was residing! See Acts the 2nd chapter verses 8 thru 10. These verses state that Jews from every nation under heaven came up to Jerusalem to keep Pentecost and mention Cyrene and Libya. Libya is the ancient name for Africa. **As you can see from this ancient map of Strabo 15 A.D, (page 15), there were only 3 continents listed; Europe (EUROPA) Asia and Libya (AFRICA).** Libya was the ancient name of Africa so go back and read your history books, the Lord had Peter to write that Israel not only resided in Libya or Africa but that Israelite children had been born in the land of Africa!

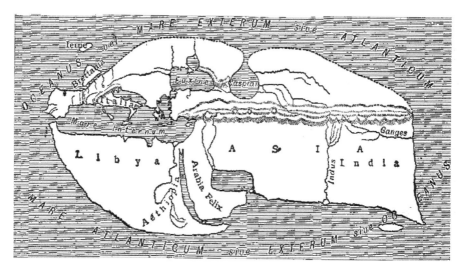

ANCIENT MAPS LIBYA IS ANCIENT NAME OF AFRICA

STRABO A.D 15 The map on page 16 is from Herodotus the famed historian 450 B.C and in his map **Libya is the name of the continent that this generation calls Africa. You should have noted that the ancients only knew of three continents and there was no such thing as a continent or a place called Africa.** This is the reason why your understanding of history is of the extreme importance, the Lord had it written in the book of Acts that Israelites lived and were born in Libya or Africa.

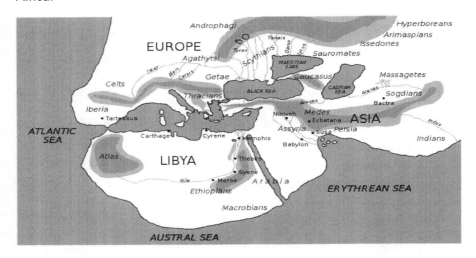

LIBYA THE NAME OF AFRICA IN THE DAYS OF JESUS & APOSTLES

Even in the days of the Apostle Peter, Israel had mingled himself among the sons of Ham but before I precede any further I shall provide you with further proof that Israel had no problem living among the sons of Ham. See Ezra the 9th chapter verses 1 and 2; it states that Israel had mingled among the Canaanites, Hittites, Perizittes, Jebusites, Ammonites, Moabites, Egyptians, and the Amorites. These are all the black tribes or black sons of Ham. You can find them listed as Ham's sons in the Tenth chapter of Genesis. Now for the question of the last 2000 years where is the proof that Israel is among the African nations? **It's interesting that the writers of the new translations of the Bible never considered informing the readers that Libya is the ancient name of Africa,** can this be mere coincidence? In fact, when the first Negros came into Virginia in

1619, I believe there were 9 to 16 persons. Since that time (392 long years later) 42 million Negroes have been born in this American captivity. Think for a moment, not only have children been born to the Negro in this captivity, the Negro has also mingled with the people of the land. The black man in America has married the Japanese, Pekinese, Chinese, Europeans and basically every race of women he has come in contact with! He hasn't changed in 6000 years! Below is an image of a group of Mesopotamian black men and African black men, can you tell the difference?

The man taking the beating is a black Hebrew Israelite and the men giving the beating are black Egyptians. The men with the colored clothing on are none other than black Hebrew Israelite taken from the tomb of Beni Hassan in Egypt. Notice the Hebrew Israelite holding the writing tablet, it reads these are the people of God! The black men to your extreme right are black Canaanites. If I hadn't told you, there was no way you could have known and this is the problem with the mingling of the races, especially if they look just alike! This is the problem that the North Atlantic slave trade presented to the historian of this current generation, who is the Hebrew (Mesopotamian) and who is the Hammite (African). There was a Hebrew colony at Carthage and its leader was black Hannibal! Hannibal depicted himself as a black man not the writer.

COIN: HANNIBAL OF CARTHAGE

COIN FOUND IN CLANIS VALLEY, ITALY

207 B.C TO 217 B.C

CHAPTER 2   ISRAELITE COLONIES

Carthage (AFRICA) was a Jewish colony founded in North Africa in the year 800 B.C by the black Phoenicians. It could have been a place of refuge for the Israelites fleeing the Assyrian invasion of 722 B.C. See 2nd Kings the entire 17th chapter. Carthage was defeated by the Romans in 201 B.C, by the Roman General Scipio Africanus. Libya was named after this roman general Africanus and this is where the name Africa came from. Most Negros hasn't taken the time out to learn this simple fact while they style themselves African Americans.

Cyrene (AFRICA) not much is known of Cyrene (in Africa) but we do know black Jews were born here according to the Apostle Peter in the 2nd chapter of Acts and some of the prophets and teachers came from there according to Acts 13:1, and the close proximity to the Nile river would make this a quick get away if you were fleeing the Assyrian horde.

We also know that it has been recorded **that the Cyrenaica Jews revolted in 115 A.D under the Romans**, and that it ceased to exist after the Arab invasion in 640 A.D.

ALEXANDRIA (AFRICA) history states that **the black Jews of Alexandria** were present with the founding of this city by Alexander the Great in 332B.C. History also records that the city was wiped out by the Roman Trajan during the Jewish revolt in 115-117 A.D

ELEPHANTINE (Africa): as late as 494 B.C documents show that this Jewish community had a temple at Elephantine and a temple to YHWH (JEHOVAH) and that some of the people were soldiers.

Memphis (Africa): much is known about the fact that Jeremiah the Prophet and the kings seed sought refuge in Egypt (which is in Africa) see Jeremiah the 43rd chapter verses 1-7 and Jeremiah the 44th chapter verses 1-3. Egypt was overrun by the Arabs under the Caliphs in 640 A.D.

Jerusalem (Northeast Africa: hard to believe huh?): home of the black Hebrews the seed of Shem was overrun by the Romans in 70 A.D then by the Arabs in 640 A.D.

See the map below, take note of Carthage, Cyrene, Alexandria, Elephantine and Memphis were all Jewish

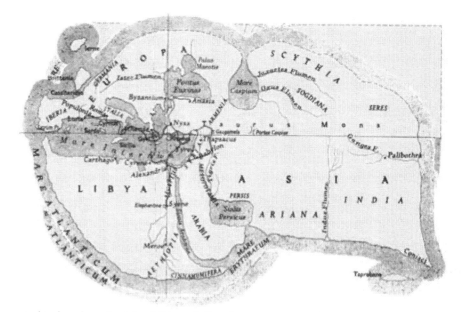

colonies located in Africa (Libya), not to mention Israel in northeast Africa. Also the bible states that the inhabitants that remained in Judah after Nebuchadnezzar destroyed Jerusalem took refuge in Taphanes which is in Egypt. Let's do a brief recap, what do we have so far? So far, we've proven that there were black Jews and black Mesopotamians who looked just like black Africans. Then next we proved that there were black Jewish colonies in Egypt Africa. Before I go any further I would like to mention the migration of peoples, it is common knowledge among the so called historians of this generation that all the peoples of the world have migrated over the last 6000 years from time to time.

Case in point, the migration of Caucasian people. It is a known fact that when Attila crossed the Volga in the 5th century that you had one of the greatest migrations of Europeans **(the barbarians)** that any generation had ever witnessed, the **Goths, Vandals, Ostrogoths and the Visigoths.** All of these tribes crossed over into the Roman Empire causing the fall of Rome! This was the beginning of what the Gentiles call The Dark Ages. This was the same period in which the Jutes, Angles and Saxons, (Barbarians from Northern Europe) this modern day English man or Britain, invaded Roman Britain by ships and they have been there ever since! This is the reason they call themselves Anglo Saxon, go back and read your history books you will be surprised! Not to mention the migration (COLONIZING) of whites into the Americas, Australia, Europe, Africa, and India. It is interesting that Europeans can migrate but people of color cannot and not only are black folk not permitted to migrate they can't even migrate in their own backyard. Let's look at some of the tribes in Africa who claim to be Israelites and some of the dates affixed to them. We know that Jerusalem was attacked and destroyed by Nebuchadnezzar in waves between 606 B.C and finally 587 B.C. There is a tribe that is situated by the Niger River which evolved into an empire called the Ashanti, which used to be ancient Ghana. Let's investigate their story.

CHAPTER 3   ISRAEL IN AFRICA

When Joshua is handing out the inheritance to the children of Israel he begins to give Judah his inheritance, see Joshua the 15th chapter beginning with verse 20-42, emphasis on verse 42 because to the tribe of Judah was given the city **Ashan.** Next run to Joshua 19: 7, to Simeon was given an inheritance in **Ashan**. Next, let's examine **1 Chronicles 6:50-59** to the Levite was given an inheritance in **Ashan** with her suburbs. So we have here 3 tribes mentioned in the bible whose dwelling was in Ashan, in the land of Judah. There was a tribe located in west Nigeria called **the Ashanti, the ti denoting the people of Ashan.** Historically the Ashanti Empire fought wars against the British Kidnapping Empire and won some and lost some. SEE MAP OF ASHANTI EMPIRE ON NEXT PAGE!

MAP OF ASHANTI EMPIRE

But there is a picture taken from the London times in the year 1848 by Sir Henry M Stanley, this picture shows an Ashanti priest crossing the Prah river in Nigeria, with a cap on his head, which reads holy to YHWH and a breastplate on his chest with 12 stones in it. See the image below!

ASHANTI PRIEST CROSSING PRAH RIVER IN NIGERIA

BREASTPLATESTONES: The breastplate and bonnet can be found in the law of Moses. See **Exodus 28:1, 2, 4, 9, 10, 11, 12, 17, 18, 19, 20, 21** the **breastplate**, two onyx stones and the names of the **12 tribes of Israel**. The circumcising of the sons on the 8th day, see Genesis 17: 1, 2, 9, 10,11,12,13. The circumcision was given to Abraham as an everlasting covenant and the so called barbaric tribes of Africa embraced the Covenant of the Almighty! This is indisputable evidence of a great cover up, that the Europeans knew who we were as early as 1800 A.D and have deliberately hidden the truth from 42 million so called Negros! This would also mean the Ashanti priest had knowledge of the scriptures before they came to the shores of the Americas! What happened to the Ashanti? The Anglo-Ashanti wars were four conflicts between **the Ashanti Empire**, the Akan interior of what are now Ghana and **the British Empire** in the 19th century between 1824 and 1901. The first Anglo-Ashanti War between the two empires **(the key words are Black Ashanti Empire)** was from 1823 to 1831 where Sir Charles McCarthy and Ensign Wetherall were defeated and killed by the Ashanti and their heads were kept as trophies. In 1832 the Pra river was accepted as the border in a treaty and there were thirty years of peace. The second Anglo-Ashanti war was from 1863 to 1864 a large delegation of Ashanti crossed the Pra river seeking a fugitive, the British refused to relinquish the person and there was fighting with casualties on both sides. The 3rd Anglo-Ashanti war lasted from 1873 to 1874. In 1874 the British purchased the Dutch Gold Coast from the Dutch including Elmina which was claimed by the Ashanti. The Ashanti invaded the new British protectorate. The war was covered by Henry Morton Stanley and G.A Henty. This time the Ashanti lost and by the time the Ashanti fourth war it was all but over for the Ashanti Empire. Yaa Asante is the queen mother of the Ashanti; she was the one to lead the 4th war against the British. Asantehe Prempeh shown below was a feared Ashanti king.

QUEEN YAA ASANTE

KING PREMPEH1

Notice the name of the queen of the Ashanti She was named after the God of Israel YAA or as the book of Psalms spelled it JAH, see Psalm 68:4 . Make no mistake about it our fathers on the other side of the Atlantic worshipped YHWH. Later in this book we will show you how the Angle Saxon Jute gave the Negro his gods, his diet and his holydays! As you can see from this map below that the Ashanti were sold (GOLD COAST) as captives first in South America, and then in North America. How do I know? It has been recorded that the Ashanti or Korromante were so rebellious that the Spanish and French would not permit them into their colonies and that there was only one market open to them and that market was the British colonies. That means the people of Ashan, the tribes of **Simeon, Judah, and Levi** are in **South America** and right here in the **United States of America**. Think about this hard and long, if I can see this and I didn't major in any form of history in college (my major was Accounting), why can't the professors of the prestigious universities in America see this? How come your Pastors be they white, yellow, brown or black can't see this? Did they not go to Seminary college? Oh I forgot the Seminary colleges teach the doctrine of Rome. **Jesus said",** when the Holy Ghost comes he will lead you teach you and guide you". See the map of the North Atlantic slave trade on the next page.

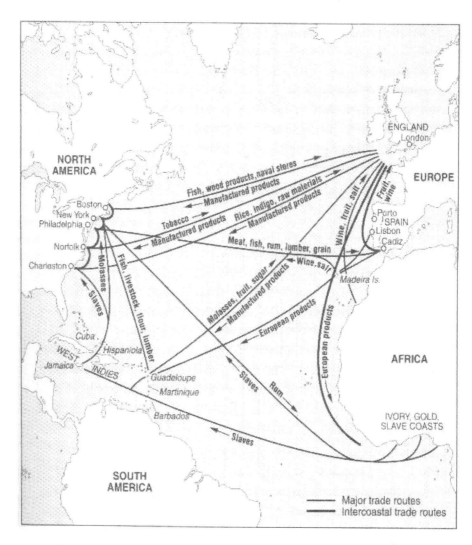

BLACK HEBREW ISRAELITES THE ASHANTEE, GO INTO MIDDLE PASSAGE AND NORTH AMERICAN CAPTIVITY!
Barbados, Bahamas, Jamaica, Cuba, Indies, Guadeloupe, Hispaniola and all of South America & Central America

Here is another tantalizing item that can't be dismissed we have a letter written from the Ashanti queen to the queen of England where she states that the Ashanti serve the great God Nyankopon, on whom men lean and do not fall, **whose day of worship is Saturday, and whom the Ashanti serve!!** See Hebrewisms of west Africa page 54, Joseph J Williams. If you are a true student of history you will remember that the ancient Druids were the priests of the ancient Celts, of whom the modern day British or Englishman descended from. These Druid priests taught the ancient Celts the worship of the sun god Baal. This is where all the Protestant churches and Catholic Churches get their worshipping on Sunday from and these are ancient things. The thing that you should make a note of is the Ashanti was worshipping the God of Israel, keeping the Sabbath day, circumcising their sons on the 8th day and keeping the holydays long before the missionaries of the kidnapping Europeans ever made it to Africa! You have to get this in your mind and remember that from 1619 the Negro in America was not permitted to read or write. If that is the case and it is, who taught the Negro his form of religion? The Roman Catholic Church sprinted down to the slave quarters and forced fed our fathers their religion. **The same church that closed their eyes to our fathers sufferings!**

Next, we will turn our attention to the Igbo Jews of Nigeria. The Igbo are said to have migrated from Syria and Libya into West Africa. Historical records show this migration started around 640 A.D when the Arabs under the Caliphs attacked Syria. The tribes that migrated were **Dan, Naphtali, Gad, and Asher** which resettled in Nigeria and became known **as the Sambatyon Jews**. In the years **1484 and 1667 Judeans and Zebulonians from Portugal and Libya joined Sambatyon Jews of Nigeria** Jews. This was taken from the work of Chinedu Nwabunwanne of Aguleri, a professor at the University of UCLA. This would also mean that the brothers had knowledge of who they were as early as 1484! See port of entry on next page.

IGBO WOMEN ATTENDING A WEDDING

PORT OF ENTRY OF EUROPEAN KIDNAPPERS

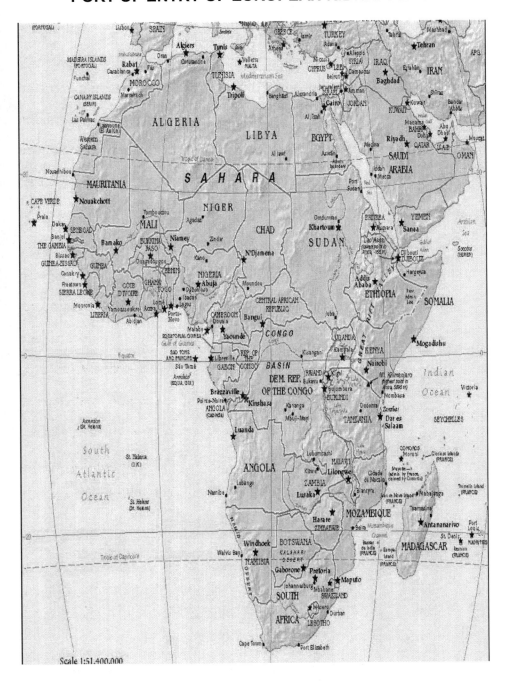

What are the implications of such history? We know that the Nigerians were sold into this captivity because of the one word Negros despise the most, NIGGER. This word can be found on any map of Africa as NIGER, a word that denotes the location on the Gold Coast where Negros was kidnapped from. This means that **the tribes of Dan, Naphtali, Gad, Judah and Zebulon are in the Americas'**, joining the **tribe of LEVI, the Ashanti**. This has brought to pass that old prophecy in the book of Genesis 49:10, "the scepter shall not depart from **Judah,** or the lawgiver (LEVI) from between his feet Judah and Levi are together here in the United States! Here is a picture of these Sambatyan Jews of Nigeria. These guys look like guys you see everyday walking in the hood. They look like brothers from the ghettos in Chicago, NewYork, Philadelphia, Los Angeles, and Pittsburgh, Washington. Our minds had been seared with a hot iron, what does that mean? We had our memory erased through the lack of knowledge but now God has decided it is time for us to remember who we are because the 2nd return of Christ is at hand.

SAMBATYAN JEWS OF NIGERIA

These Nigerian Jews gained official status in 1995-1997 when Israeli Prime Minister Yitzhak Rabin sent a team to Nigeria in search of the Ten Lost Tribes of Israel. This statement reeks of stupidity and I'll explain why, it is common knowledge among those in the know that on January 4, 1985 there was a secret airlift of Ethiopian Jews into the land of Israel.

ETHIOPIAN JEWS BEING AIRLIFTED TO ISRAEL

Also Operation Solomon took place in 1991 bringing 14,000 Ethiopian Jews to Israel, culminating with the arrival of about 40,000 Ethiopian Jews. The scene with the Ethiopian Jews being airlifted to Israel reminds me of the scripture concerning the gathering of Israel. See Isaiah 60:8, who are these that fly as a cloud, and as the doves to their windows? This isn't ancient history, you don't have to dig in the ground to find this information this is practically a current event! Didn't the Lord have the prophet Amos to write, Amos 9:7, **art not you as the children** of Ethiopia unto me and in another place, Jeremiah 13:23 can the Ethiopian change his skin or a leopard his spots?

 The tribe of Dan to prove their antiquity and authenticity of their own claims, the Beta Israel cite the 9th century testimony of Eldad ha dani (the Danite), from a time before even the Zagwean dynasty was established. Eldad was a Jewish man of dark skin who suddenly turned up in Egypt and created a great stir in the Egyptian Jewish community (and elsewhere in the Mediterranean Jewish communities he travelled to) with claims that he had come from a Jewish kingdom of pastoralists far to the south. The only language he spoke was a hitherto unknown dialect of Hebrew. Although he strictly followed the Mosaic commandments his observance differed in some details from rabbinic halakhah, so that some thought he might be a Karaite, even if his practice differed from theirs too. He carried Hebrew books with him that supported his explanations of halakhah, and he was able to cite ancient authorities in the sagely traditions of his own people. He said that the Jews of his own kingdom derived from the tribe of Dan, which had fled the civil war in the Kingdom of Israel between Solomon's son Rehoboam and Jeroboam the son of Nebat, by resettling in Egypt. From there they moved southwards up the Nile into

Ethiopia, and the Beta Israel say this confirms that they are descended from these Danites. Some Beta Israel however, assert even nowadays that their Danite origins go back to the time of Moses himself, when some Danites parted from other Jews right after the Exodus and moved south to Ethiopia. Eldad the Danite does indeed speak of at least three waves of Jewish immigration into his region, creating other Jewish tribes and kingdoms, including the earliest wave that settled in a remote kingdom of the tribe of Moses. This was the strongest and most secure Jewish kingdom of all, with farming villages, cities and great wealth. The Mosaic claims of the Beta Israel, in any case, like those of the Zagwe dynasty itself, are clearly very ancient. Sources tell of many Jews who were brought as prisoners of war from ancient Israel by Ptolemy I and also settled on the border of his kingdom with Nubia (Sudan). Another tradition handed down in the community from father to son asserts that they arrived either via the old district of Qwara in northwestern Ethiopia, or via the Atbara River, where the Nile tributaries flow into Sudan. Some accounts even specify the route taken by their forefathers on their way upstream from Egypt. The Beta Israelites lived in north and northwestern Ethiopia. Nearly 120,000 of these black Ethiopian Jews have been allowed to return to Israel under **operation Moses 1984, operation Sheba 1985** and of course the aforementioned **operation Solomon 1991**. The white Jews in Israel are flawed in that they think they have a monopoly on who is Israel and who isn't. The Lord told Moses that Israel would be scattered into every nation under the sun and Africa has today 54 nations. A bit of world history demands a place in this book. There was a secret meeting among the European colonizing nations in Europe called the Belgium conference presided over by King

Leopold of Belgium (known as the butcher) in the year 1884. This meeting that was held was to decide the fate of 53 African nations. Of great interest is that none of the African nations were invited. The reason for the snub was that the Europeans had decided to carve Africa up among themselves to steal the raw materials and goods and this began the period of Globalization oops my bad, I meant colonization! The only nation not to be colonized was Ethiopia. You see Napoleon Bonaparte had bankrupted Europe with the Napoleonic wars and these Europeans were in an economic recession and they figured lets make Africa pay for it and so they did. The only nation that wasn't colonized was Ethiopia with thanks in large part to King Haile Salassie. Ethiopia had to remain black, because it was written in Amos 9:7 Art not thou as the Ethiopian unto me and Jeremiah 13:23 can the Ethiopian change his spots? The Greeks called the Ethiopians burnt face, this is how black he was and he had to remain black for a generation to come, and that generation is 2011. For the sake of our young people I put a picture of an authentic black king **(Haile Selassie)** who the Europeans and the naysayers cannot deny that has lived and was black! This will prove to our children that we once were kings and that our current state of affairs is not indicative of who we are!

KING HAILE SELASSIE OF ETHIOPIA

King Haile Selassie 1 (traces his lineage back to Solomon the son of David) went before the league of nations (the European colonizing nations) to plead the cause of his people after Benito Mussolini and the Italian people invaded Ethiopia using chemical warfare. His speech at the League of Nations has been regarded as one of the greatest speeches in the 20th century. This is an interesting fact, did you know that the colonizing European nation members that appeared at the Belgium conference in 1888 were the same good old boy European nations who started the League of Nations in 1927 and who were the same good old boy nations who started the United Nations in 1948? Guess who was not invited to sit down at the round table (membership) on all three occasions? Yes, 53 African nations, the United Nations didn't include Africa until the African Nationalists on the continent cleaned out all of the European thieves in 1960. I guess if I'm going to steal your land and your goods it would be unwise to have you at the meeting!

THE.NRI.TRIBE.OF.NIGERIA

"NRI KINGDOM is the oldest Kingdom in Nigeria. It was founded around 900AD by the progenitor, Eri, the son of Gad. According to biblical accounts, Jacob had Leah as his wife who begot four sons for him. When Leah noticed she had passed child-bearing age, she gave her maid - servant, Zilpah to Jacob to wife, and through Zilpah he had a son named Gad. **Gad then bigot Eri,** who later formed a clan known as **Erites,** see Genesis Chapter 30 verse 9; 46 verse 16 and Numbers chapter 26 verses 15-19. Eri was therefore amongst the twelve tribes of Israel via Gad. During their stay in Egypt Eri became the high priest and spiritual adviser to Pharaoh Teti the 5th dynastic Pharaoh of EGYPT IN 2400 B.C. The NRI trace their lineage back to Eri the son of Gad. And upon closer inspection of the tribe a temple was found with the inscription holy to Gad and an onyx stone with **Gads name written in ancient Hebrew**. According to Igbo lore of the Eri, Nri, and Ozubulu families the Jewish Igbo ethnic groups are comprised of the following 3 lineage types:**Benei Gath**: Igbos said to have descended from tribe of Gath ben-Ya`aqov, who was the 8th son of the Israeli patriarch Ya`aqov (Jacob). This lineage is traced though Gath's son Eri ben-Gath. The clans said to come from this lineage comprise of the Aguleri, Umuleri, Oreri, Enugwu Ikwu, Ogbunike, Awkuzu, Nteje, and

Igbariam.Benei Zevulun:

Igbos said to have descended from the tribe of Zevulun ben-Ya`aqov, who was the 5th son of Ya`aqov (Jacob). This lineage comprises of the Ubulu Okiti, Ubulu Ukwu, in Delta State, who settled in Ubulu Ihejiofor. According to tradition, it is said that a descendent of the tribe of Zevulun (ZEBULUN) named Zevulunu, on the advice of an certain Levite, married a woman from Oji, whom descended from the tribe of Judah, and from this union was born Ozubulu ben-Zebulunu. It is said that Ozubulu then went on to have 4 sons of his own who settled into other parts of the region. These sons being: Amakwa, from whom a clan in Neni, anambra state descended and Egbema , from whom the Egbema Ugwuta clan in Imo State and the Ohaji Egbema clan in Rivers state desecended Benei Menash: of whom descended the tribe of Manasah. Could this be the reason that the original homeland that the Europeans had sought for the white Jews was Africa (ancient Libya) before they settled on Palestine? They knew that the black Jews were spread out all of the interior of Africa and since the white Jew stated he was a Jew he should be comfortable with his brothers, but he isn't. That's why the Lord had it written that Israel is like a speckled bird because he will come in many shades and colors. Lets take a closer look at Manasah of the Bible.

Ben Yoseph, who was one of the grandsons of Ya`aqov (Jacob) through his 11th son Yoseph (Joseph). According to the Torah Jacob claimed both Manassah and his brother Ephrayim as his own sons. It is theorized by some that this is the possible lineage of the Amichi, Ichi, Nnewi-Ichi clans. Here is a map below showing the location of Nigeria, you should notice that east of Nigeria is the Bight of Benin (Bight- a bay that 400 miles long) it has been estimated that over one million

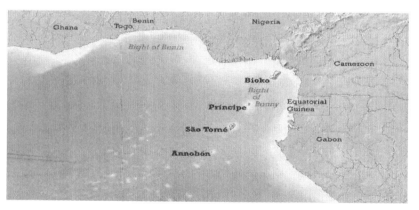

Igbos were transported from this area to Virginia, Kentucky, and Maryland. It is said that 60% of all African Americans have at least one Igbo ancestor! The word Okra, is an Igbo word.

THE LEMBA TRIBE OF SOUTH AFRICA

IMAGE OF LEMBA MEN AT SABBATH SERVICE

Tudor Parfitt a protagonist of the NOVA DOCUMENTARY, The Lost Tribes of Israel, made a trip to South Africa to study the Lemba tribe and their traditions. He wrote that he observed their customs of keeping the Sabbath, not eating blood in their foods, their keeping of the dietary law, and circumcising of their sons on the 8th day. Based on these observations Mr. Parfitt came to the conclusion that the Lemba people's customs were Semitic and not Hamitic (African). I liked this guys work to the max but he failed to mention one thing and that is that the Lemba history. The Lemba have been keeping the Law of circumcision and other Hebraic customs for thousands of years. In fact when the white missionaries came to Africa they already knew about Jesus. In order to prove or disprove the assertions of the Lemba tribe he undertook a venture with the Center for Genetic Anthropology in London.

They identified a Y chromosome marker on Lemba males and compared that to Bantu Africans, Yemini Arabs, Sephardic Jews, Askenazi Jews and the Cohanim. NOVA team Dr. David Goldstein commented the the Lemba Y (Bubba clan) chromosome was a match with the Cohen chromosome identified in the Jewish priesthood! Also of particular interest is the fact that they sought out **Bantu Africans**. Lets deviate for a moment, as you might have not known there are about **250 Bantu place names in South Carolina. Bantu speaking people were found in Angola, Rwanda, Burundi, Zimbabwe and South Africa**. The Bantu speaking people of Angola were first brought to Brazil by the Portugese. There was research done by **Dr. Joseph P Holloway** a professor at California State University at Northridge which provides extremely useful information. He found Bantu place names in Alabama, Georgia, Florida , Mississipi, North Carolina, South Carolina and Virginia. What does this mean? **It's quite simple, it proves that black Jews associated with the Lemba tribe (Bantu speaking people) were held captive in the south and that upon the great migration of Negros from 1910 to 1930 and the years 1940 to 1970 these black Jews saturated the northern cities** like Chicago, Philadelphia, Washington, Detroit, Indiana, Wisconsin, and so forth.

REPLICA ARK OF COVENANT FOUND IN ZIMBABWE 700 YEARS OLD

This reminded me of when the children of Israel were parcelling out the land of Canaan in Joushua 22: 9-34. The tribes on the other side of Jordan built an altar to the Lord and this was their logic, vereses 21,26 the tribe of Ruben, Gad and the half tribe of Manasseh stated that the reason they built the facsimile altar was so that the other tribes could not boast one day that they were not Israelites.

This image of the replica ark of the covenant that was found in South Africa reeks of the same reasoning, it appears that our fathers left relics behind to remind us of who we really were!

CHAPTER 4   THE SHIPS OF BABEL

INTERPRETED: THE SHIPS OF CONFUSION

I named this chapter the ships of Babel, because Babel means confusion and when the kidnappers of black human flesh brought in the blacks of Africa they were confused into thinking that since everybody was black that they were all African. In Genesis Chapter11: verse 9 **therefore is the name of it called Babel because the Lord did there confound** the language of all the earth and from thence did the Lord scatter them abroad upon the face of all the earth. In Deuteronomy 28:68 the Lord said he would bring Israel back into Egypt on ships and this is exactly what happened to the Negro, he came into captivity on ships. **Notice all of these blacks, some Egyptians, some Canaanites, some Elamites, some Hebrews, and some Arabs, in the same ship. Can you tell the African (Ham) from the Hebrew (Shem)?**

This is the point that I am trying to make is the European kidnapper couldn't make the distinction between the black African (son of Ham) and the black Mesopotamian (black Hebrew Israelite). On the next page I have a special treat for you, it is a $100 dollar confederate bill depicting the so called Negro hoeing and picking cotton. I bet you didn't know that the Negro was once on the face of American money did you? **See the next page.**

1861 CONFEDERATE $100 BILL SHOWING NEGRO CAPTIVES PICKING COTTON

The white establishment can never say they didn't make merchandise of the Negro because he put the Negro on his confederate money as a propaganda tool. The black Israelite captive was brought to America via the southern gate (the south) but remember there was a great migration of Negros from the South to the North from 1910 to 1930. Plus another migration took place from 1940 to 1970 relocating over 5 million Negros from the brutality of the south. It is quite simple and apparent that the black Jews of Africa are right here in the United States of America. There is a curse and prophecy written in the book of Moses actually Deuteronomy the 32nd chapter and the 68th verse which states that Israel would go back into Egypt on ships as bond men and bond women and that Israel would not see the land again. **There is no other nation on earth that went into bondage on ships but us.** It happened in A.D 70 when we were carted off to Rome under Vespasian Caesar and his son Titus Caesar and it happened again in 1619 when the first black Hebrew Israelite came into Jamestown, Virginia. See Deuteronomy 28:46, and they (curses) shall be on upon thee for a sign and for a wonder and upon thy seed for ever! Why did the Lord use the verbiage on you for a sign? Because a sign can talk, the Lord knew that when the Negro got out of this hard bondage he wouldn't even know how to read, which is the basics of civilization going back to the cuneiform tablets found in ancient Sumer. So in the process of time after he regained some of his former abilities like reading, the Lord expected the Negro to see himself in the various signs he left written in the scriptures! The Negro was supposed to be quickened by the signs but there are other forces at work keeping him in darkness. Television, radio, sports, newspapers, concerts, parties, drinking, getting high, selling drugs, gang banging, all of these things are keeping 42 million Negros in America from waking up! There was a time during slavery that the Negro would risk his life and limb to learn how to read but now he has been reduced to a Willie Lynch state. This is the condition of the entire earth right now. Case in point, when the uprisings occurred in Egypt the Mubarak regime cut off the internet, texting and cell phones in Egypt. This happened in Egypt, Libya, and Bahrain. This is the ideology (Thinking) of the power structure in this world. The Bible said," the people perish for lack of knowledge", and this has become very evident with the actions of the nations. Right here in America our government is trying to place the internet under the security act. That means that they will have the power in times of national interest to shut it down! Through the World Wide Web the Earth has become one big neighbourhood, what happens in one nation overnight is heard around the world the same night! The Chinese are no different than the Arab nations who have suppressed the 1% with the shutting down of social media. In China the people are in darkness, they have a 2010 Nobel Peace Prize winner by the name of Liu Xiaobo but he has been censored, meaning the people of China don't even know he won the award! Via the internet we have access to all the libraries and history of the world uncensored by the ruling governments of the world. The powers that be are afraid of you obtaining knowledge because as your knowledge increases the vail of darkness falls off of your eyes and you can see. All over Arabia, in nations revolting the regimes are cutting off the internet, text messaging and tweeting. Open up your mind and see if the method to control and deceive 42 million Negros can work over a 392 year period why not do it to the whole world? This is how the elite maintain control over the masses, truly knowledge is power. The mindset is if you can keep the Negro in darkness he will be our servants forever, this was the mindset among the Southern white slave owners. This is the condition that the Negro community finds itself in today in America, educated in the educational institutions of the west, but educated in what? The grammar schools, high schools, and colleges in the United States have been set up for one thing to teach entire generations lies and to indoctrinate them into the history about European nations and white people, **this is the first law of darkness**. Hide a mans truth about himself from himself and then teach him the history of the **(European)** oppressor every time he shows up for schooling. Teach him to hate everything about himself and anybody that looks like him!

BLACK HEBREW ISRAELITES ARRIVE ON THE SHORES OF AMERICA 1619

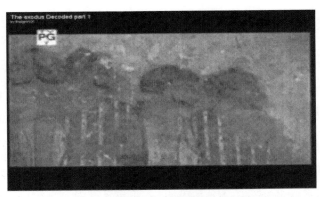

THE TABLET READS THE PEOPLE OF AMO
INTERPRETED THESE ARE THE PEOPLE OF GOD

These images were taken from the tomb of Beni Hassan in Egypt. These are images of the ancient black Hebrew Israelites going into Egypt notice the men, women and children are black, the men have afros and beards. On the second row of pictures the last one to the right the black Hebrew is holding out a tablet that reads the people of Amo". Once the tablet was interpreted it reads, "the people of God! In the book of Isaiah, the 49th chapter verse 15 reads, can a woman forget her sucking child, that she should not have compassion on the son of her womb: year , they may forget yet will I not forget thee. Verse 16 behold I have graven thee upon the palms of my hands; thy walls are continually before me. The God of Israel hid all of this information concerning the true people of Israel in tombs and pyramids from those who destroyed the pictures of the prophets and the apostles. Think for a moment when Jesus took Peter, James and John with him up into the mount where he was transfigured before them it was written that the apostles recognized Moses and Elijah. This would imply that they had seen pictures of the elders because Moses and Elijah lived almost 2000 years before the apostles had ever been born! The only image we have that names an elder is the coin with Joseph's image and name on it recently released by the Arab government ruling in Egypt. In fact I'm not sure these Arabs in Arabia are indeed Arab because they don't look like the black Arabs of Arabia. The History channel did a special on the pyramids of Egypt and stumbled on this truth but it wasn't emphasized during the special. The sight of these images and the interpretation of the writing tablet blew me away but notice something else. The truth has been locked up behind bars! These are the people that came into the North Atlantic Slave Trade the Amo, or the people of God who have been bitterly mistreated by the Europeans. Once our fathers arrived here in America we were sold as chattel . See Deuteronomy 28: 49, 50, 68 you need to read the entire chapter to get some understanding. The Lord had it written that the nation that would take us back into captivity would have the eagle as its standard (America) and that Israel would be sold as bondmen and bondwomen.

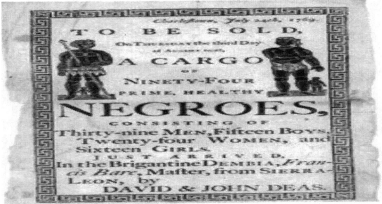

That is why I was extremely amused by the propaganda of the 70's and 80's where it was said that black women didn't need a black man. If you are a black woman reading this book remember this, you are still a part of the Negro struggle whether you believe it or not. The fate of the black woman and child is woven together with the fate of the black man! When you get some time o black woman and o black man read the book of Esther the 3rd and 4th chapter, in the 4th chapter of Esther the 13th and 14th verse, Mordecai put it very bluntly to Esther and told her don't think you will escape because of your position in the kingdom. I am saying the same thing to you sisters and brothers in the corporate sector: Don't fool yourself, you have been included in the total Negro Census no matter what your status is in America, 42 million, and you are still part of the Negro question! How was the European able to keep a strong people like the Negro in captivity? 1818: A letter from "Judex" (a court arbitrator) in Leesburg's *Genius of Liberty*, warns **that teaching slaves to read and write is illegal**. "Negroes, teachers and justices look to it: the order of society must prevail over the notions of individuals." The sons of the Empire were not simply imprisoned in America, the Negro was placed in complete darkness, the kind of darkness you see when you enter his penal system, the darkness of the mind! If you have young Negros in your home, in your family, please get them this book as it will begin to answer a lot of questions in their minds concerning the condition that he finds himself in America.

The first law of Darkness has been amended by the elite, the amendment to the law: it is okay in this generation for the Negro to learn how to read and write as long as he is reading information that we provide for him (indoctrination). This means we can still control him without the physical chains of bondage. You see the new chains will be the chaining of his mind, feed him European history, teach him nothing about himself, take the Negro champions of history and make them white so the Negro will think he had never accomplished anything. Make the Negro think his history began in 1619 with the coming of the kidnappers!

CHAPTER 5   THE NEGRO RESISTANCE

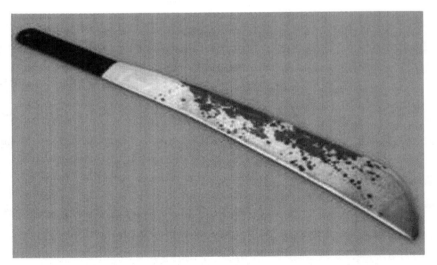

The Europeans would have the children of the Empire to believe that our fathers did not put up a fight for their wives, sons and daughters. I will show you that the Negro fought for his freedom.

L overture Toussaint

Toussaint was a captive in Haiti and led a revolt defeating a sizeable British, Spanish and America force, of about 10,000 men. Toussaint became governor for life and freed the slaves of San Domingo. He made the mistake of making a trip to France to meet Napoleon, for peace. When he arrived he was arrested, placed in a dungeon and there he died in 1803. When the Hebrew Israelite captives heard of the exploits of Toussaint they were encouraged.

NAT TURNER   THE YEAR 1831

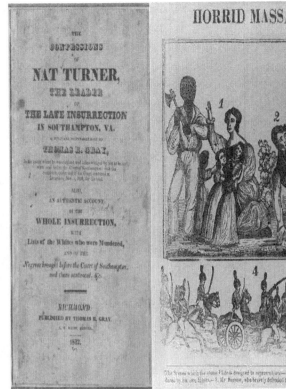

This article is amusing because these Anglo, Saxon, Jutes (white Americans) called what Nat Turner did murder and the second article called it a horrid massacre. These people had been raping, murdering and dismembering the Negro captive since his arrival in hell, 392 years, and they never thought for one minute that these good Negros would snap! It is the old bully syndrome, the guy is beating you up, taking your money, insulting you in front of your woman everytime he sees you. Then one day you get it in your mind that ," i've had about enough of this" and when you see the bully you give him the beating that his parents never gave him! This could have been the mindset of the negro men that went on that mission with Nat turner one hundred and eighty years ago. Nat Turner went from farm to farm killing white Americans he and a few Negros he had recruited. **The young people have a rap song that says, " it ain't no fun whern the rabbit has the gun"**. These were the actions of a free man, according to the Bible if any man is caught stealing another man he shall be stoned to death.

NEW YORK SLAVE REBELLION 1712

25 Negro captives armed with guns and clubs killed 9 whites and burned down homes before being killed.

CATO STONO REBELLION 1739

80 Negro captives armed themselves marching toward Spanish Florida. A battle ensued killing 42 Blacks and 21 Whites. We could mention Gabriel Prosser, Denmark Vessey, the Fort Blunt rebellion and over 200 insurrections and rebellions. The white educational system in the United States teaches our children that the elders

went along with the program and this is historically a lie! Slaves don't jump overboard ships in the North Atlantic to be eaten by sharks, slaves don't starve themselves to death, slaves don't run away, slaves won't poison the kidnapper, and lastly a slave won't sacrifice his own life. These are not the actions of a slave, these are the actions of a free man. All of these men sacrificed their lives for these people. This **propoganda** (The black elders were spineless) was designed to indoctrinate our sons into thinking that the black men didn't have any heart. The brainwashing began from the time that our fathers were shorties. The racist white kidnapper was breaking the spirits of our fathers when they became old enough to walk and talk! The same thing is happening in this generation through the American educational system. This is the real reason your sons and daughters don't want to go to school, they are not being deliberatly disobedient to you, they recognize the mental damage that is being inflicted on them through the lies they hear for 365 days every year about their forefathers. If you aren't teaching your son that he won't ever amount to anything who is? It is the American educational system, how would you feel sitting in the classroom with other ethnic groups and the only thing you ever hear about yourself is that you were a descendant of slaves, **a fat lie!**

HARRIET TUBMAN

NEWSPAPER REWARD

FOUNDER OF THE UNDERGROUND RAILROAD

After escaping slavery she completed 13 missions rescuing her family and other members of the Negro race from the hard captivity in America. She was nicknamed Moses and large rewards were issued for her arrest and whereabouts but they had no knowledge that it was her! This is the legend of the underground railroad. There is a lesson in her **(Harriet Tubman)** actions and that is when you make it out of the ghetto don't forget to reach back and help the ones left behind! I would be remiss if I didn't mention the true white christians in history who helped the Negro captive going against the cruel ideology of that generation. The news clipping to the right of Harriet Tubman is a news article about her and her 2 brothers running away and the reward for their capture and return.

SOJOURNER TRUTH
1797- 1883

A great Negro female Abolitionist who labored for the freedom of the Negro captive and once met Abraham Lincoln, she definetly has a place in the Negro hall of fame.

THE ROMAN POPES PAPAL BULLS CONDONING SLAVERY

At the time the Negro captive was suffering under the destruction of his continent, the enslavement of his wives and children one of the most powerful white institutions in the world at that time turned a deaf ear to the moans and groans of an entire continent, the Catholic church. We will show you that at least 2 Popes issued Papal Bulls condoning slavery beginning with **The Dum Diversas, issued by Pope Nicholas V**

POPE NICHOLAS THE V

PAPACY FROM 1447 – 1455

in 1452, authorized King Alfonso V of Portugal to reduce any "Saracens (Muslims) and pagans (black JEWS) and **any other**

<u>unbelievers</u>"(black Hebrew Israelites) to perpetual slavery, thereby ushering in the West African slave trade. **The Romanus Pontifex, also issued by Pope Nicholas V in 1455,** sanctioned the seizure of **non-Christian lands,** and encouraged **the enslavement of non Christian people in Africa** and the Americas. Specifically, it gave the green light to "invade, search out, capture, vanquish, and subdue all Saracens and Pagans whatsoever, and other enemies of Christ where so ever placed," all for profit, and in the name of Jesus Christ. **The Inter Caetera,** signed by **Pope Alexander VI in 1493,** states

POPE ALEXANDER THE V1

we (the Papacy) command you (Spain) ... **<u>to instruct the aforesaid</u> <u>inhabitants and residents and</u> <u>dwellers therein in the Catholic</u>**

__faith__, and train them in good morals." This papal law sanctioned and paved the way for European colonization and Catholic missions in the New World. Who were the non believers? **Remember the Ashanti, the Igbos (Jews of Nigeria) Beta Jews of Ethiopia, the Falaysha Jews, the Lemba tribe and all of the Jews in the wheat coast, the gold coast and so called slave coast of West Africa. These people worshipped the God of the Sabbath, they circumcised their sons on the 8th day, they kept the dietary law in the 11th chapter of Leviticus, they kept the blowing of trumpets and the feast days. The people of the captivity were non believers of what?** Examine the verbiage from the council of the Laodicea, it states," that Christians **must not Judaize by resting on the Sabbath day but must work on that day**, rather honoring the Lords day (Sunday) (which Lord?) if they be found resting as Christians, but if any should be found to be Judaizers let them be anathema from Christ! **This is one of the reasons why the Europeans justified enslaving the black Hebrews from West Africa because they were Judaizers!!** After all of these official documents coming from the Angle, Saxon, and Jute priest (Papacy) you have a strange event taking place in 1865. Remember under **the law of darkness**, it was illegal to teach the Negro to read or write, so who do you suppose made his way to the so called slave quarters to instruct the Negro in the ways Christ? Remember the Negro couldn't read or write under the law of darkness, so who do you think taught the Negro his religion? It was the Papacy, and the Papacy taught our fathers how to worship God contrary to the scriptures! This is why the Lord had the prophet to write this people has been robbed and spoiled. Robbed of his memory, his identity, his resting place and his God! The most high had it written in the writings of the prophet Moses, Deuteronomy 32:36, when he saw that their power is gone he would intervene and he did. Watch God in action, the Negro didn't have an army to fight on his behalf so the Lord of the Sabbath made the north and the south fight each other. This happens to be the Lords calling card to make your enemies fight each other, go with me to a scene in the bible , you will need to read the entire 20th chapter of 2 chronicles, but I shall narrarate for you. A great host came up against Jehosaphat and Judea and so the entire nation cried to the living God concerning this matter and the spirit came over the priest Azariah telling them the Lord would handle this battle. In the 20th chapter of 2nd Chronicles and the 23rd verse it reads, for the children of Ammon and Moab stood up against the inhabitants of mount Seir utterly to slay and destroy them: when they had made an end of the inhabitants of Seir, every one helped to destroy one another. This is what happened in the

Civil War the Most High had intervened on behalf of Israel and had the two brothers (the north and the south) to fight against each other. The Lord remembered his covenant with Abraham that stated he would be a God unto his seed that should come after him. This was the Lords doing and it was marvelous in his eyes but no man considered it.

The Emancipation Proclamation was the strangest of all documents, it didn't provide for reparations, it provided for 40 acres and a mule (I never got mine). It was a thankyou for everything you did, now get the hell out document, and oh by the way you'll remain in the South at the mercy of racist whites, without guns and protection until the Civil Rights Act! Then history shifts to Frederick Douglass the Negro Abolitionist.

FREDERICK DOUGLASS
1817-1895

This is the first time in modern history that the Negro question had arisen and believe it or not the Negro started the question (you means to tell me this Negro can think?) History records that three Presidents tried to answer the Negro question, Monroe, Lincoln, and Jackson. James Monroe had $100,000 appropriated for the emigration of Negroes to Liberia. Lincoln worked the hardest on the emigration of the Negro, **Lincoln had tried to secure land in South America but three nations vetoed it, Nicauraga, Honduras and Costa Rica and refused to let the Negros in his hemisphere**, may God remember these nations for this great wickedness! Frederick Douglas took a delegation of Negro elders to see Lincoln about the emigration issue, and stated unequivocally that the Negro was here to stay. My opinion in hindsight is who gave Frederick Douglas the right to speak for 4 to 5 million captive people? It has been recorded that at least 14,000 freed blacks had sent in letters expressing their intent to relocate if given the opportunity. **I am forever indebted to President Lincoln for one thing, in his communications he defined the Negro in America as a captive, not a slave.** I am of the opinion that the degrading term Slave should be stricken from all history books in America. I don't mean to villify Frederick Douglass because he too should be enshrined in the Negro hall of fame because he helped to speed up the emancipation of the negro people through his agitation. It should be very apparent to you that the Negro question has yet to be answered but as you will see later I will attempt to answer this question. The God of Israel had seen enough of the carnage and wickedness associatied with the North Atlantic slave trade and he saw the hearts of this white man concerning the so called Negro. Don't you ever forget this, that the whites in America had perpetual slavery in mind when it came to the black Jew. It was in the Willie Lynch letters and was mentioned in the Papal bulls! So they got around to giving the black man what God gave to him when he was created, freedom. If you go back and look at history the Negro was thrust out of the plantations onto the streets of the South. He was given no reparations and no land to till. This beast of burden was sent out empty handed en mass and he still couldn't read or write. So the Emancipation Proclamation made homeless

men and women out of the black Jews (Negros) And set him up to be exploited by the white capitalists in America, because he was cheap labor that couldn't read. This free Negro had no choice but to continue to till the land under the disguise of sharecropping, but because he couldn't read he never knew when he made a profit!

CHAPTER 6   THE QUARREL OF THE COVENANT

Do you remember ever going to the grocery store or the laundry mat with your mother and you did something or said something she didn't like? It could have been something as simple as a bad facial expression, and you got smacked right there in front of everybody, talk about being embarrased. To the strangers observing the discipline it looked like your mother was cruel but it was simply family business being played out in front of strangers. This is what has been going on with the black Israelite and his God over the last 2000 years, our God and our father has been chastening his children (the black Hebrew Israelite Nation) in front of the global community for the breaking of his covenant and I will prove that to you with the conditions that prevailed post slavery and even down to this generation, it was and is family business! The living God came down on Mount Sinai and affirmed the covenant he made with the seed of Abraham, Issac, and Jacob Israel. See exodus 19:17-25, I'm paraphrasing, God came down on Mount Sinai and he gave Israel his laws, statutes and his judgements and he entered into a covenant with the newly formed nation Israel. See exodus 34: 27,28 and the Lord said unto Moses, write thou these words for after the tenor of these words I have made a covenant with thee and with Israel verse 28 and he was there with the Lord forty days and forty nights he did neither eat bread nor drink water and he wrote upon the tables the words of the covenant, the Ten Commandments! What did this God look like that descended upon Mount Sinai? Lets see if the bible can answer this, run with me to Revelation the 1st chapter and verses 12,13,14,15 verse 14 **his head and his hairs**

were white like wool (not straight or stringy) as white as snow and **his eyes were as a flame of fire** (not blue eyed) verse 15 and **his feet like unto fine brass as if they burned in a furnance** (not white feet), this is the God that showed up on Mount Sinai. The question is what color did the ancient Israelites paint their God, lets see!

THE JESUS OF AFRICA

Christ and his disciples.
Painted wooden panel in the Coptic Museum, Cairo.

As you can see the coptics of Cairo Egypt painted the Christ according to the Bibles description of him but I have other witnesses than this. Examine the image on the next page, look at the dating of this fresco 1200 A.D.

Mavriótissa Monastery Narthex (northern Greece) circa 1,200 A.D. | The Last Judgement - close-up

A JUDGEMENT SCENE WITH THE SAINTS JUDGING

In every scene the ancients painted the Jesus of the Bible black, but what about the Pope? He is supposed to be God's representative on earth, isn't he? The word out of Rome is that the guy is infallible, all seeing, all knowing. I feel that if anybody should know what color Jesus is it shoud be this guy. Now I don't want you to go and get all tearied eyed about what you are about to see on the next couple of pages but what is that bible saying," you shall know the truth and the truth shall set you free". I am about to set a whole lot of you mentally free.

ONE OF THE SECRETS OF THE EUROPEANS

JOHN PAUL   POPE BENEDICT

PRAYING TO BLACK JESUS

POPE JOHN PAUL

PRAYING TO BLACK JESUS

Pope John Paul the 2nd went to visit Angola in 1992 and bowed before the image of black Jesus. Would he have done this if Jesus wasn't black? Note also to the right of John Paul you have this current Pope Benedict praying to the Black Jesus Mary image of Poland! These are the wisest most religious white men on earth, so surely they wouldn't bow before this image if Jesus is not black. Do you think that these are the only images of a black Jesus? Practically all of Europe worships a black Jesus and Mary. See images below!

BLACK JESUS CONTINUED:

JESUS OF FRANCE   JESUS OF BRAZIL   JESUS OF SPAIN

BLACK JESUS OF MEXICO

BLACK JESUS OF GUATEMALA

All over the world the nations and the Papacy recognize a black Christ but in one place, the minds of the black man in America. This people have been so thoroughly Willie Lynched by the churches and the educational institutions in the United States that they can not believe the truth. **This completes the Negro mentally as a people,** when his God looks like him and not some bearded European!

Christ and his disciples.
Painted wooden panel in the Coptic Museum, Cairo.

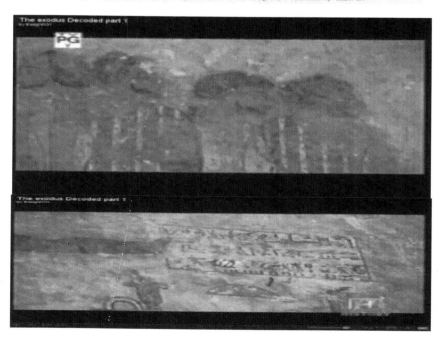

THIS TABLET READS," THE PEOPLE OF GOD!

So the people of AMO or the people of God, looked just like their God, oh my this is a surprise isn't it? The God of Israel looks just like his people. All nations paint images of their God to look like them. The only people on earth that I am acutley aware of that takes a God that dosen't look like them is this so called Negro in America! The Negro in America has been so thouroughly brainwashed by the system in this country, that to point out this simple fact makes one racist among his own kind.

THESE CURSES SHALL BE FOR A SIGN

After he had given the fathers his covenant he told the fathers that if they walked in the sins of the nations around them that they would be cursed and that these curses would be on Israel for a sign and wonder. Let's examine these curse signs and you tell me who they are pointing toward. Go with me to Deuteronomy 28:14-68, I will focus on specific scriptures or you can actually read the entire 28th chapter of Deuteronomy for enlightenment. Deuteronomy 28: 14 and thou shalt not go aside from any of the words which I command thee this day to the right hand or to the left to go after other gods to serve them. Verse 15 but it shall come to pass if thou wilt not hearken unto the voice of the lord thy God to observe to do all his commandments and his statutes which I command thee this day that all these curses shall come upon thee and overtake thee: verse 16 **cursed shalt thou be in the city and cursed shalt thou be in the field**. The so called Negro was cursed when he toiled the fields for free in the south and he was cursed under sharecropping. Then under the great migration from 1910-1930 and 1940-1970 he moved north to the cities and became a city dweller, but the curse followed him north. He couldn't find a job and he couldn't support his family, so he was cursed in the field and cursed in the city. Verse 28 the Lord shall smite thee with madness and blindness (who is blinder than the black man?) and astonishment of heart , verse 29 and thou shalt grope at noonday as the blind gropeth in darkness and thou shalt not prosper in thy ways and thou shalt be only oppressed and spoiled evermore and no man shall save thee. This 29th verse states that you will be oppressed and spoiled. **Who is more oppressed than the Negro**? Who is spoiled more than the Negro? I don't care what nation you find us in we are oppressed. Verse 37 and thou shalt become an astonishment , a proverb, and a byword among all nations where the Lord shall lead thee . What do you think the thought is that comes to other ethnic groups minds when they see how the Negro lives and conducts himself? You know what a byword is? Ex, **coon, blackie, jungle bunny, monkey, sambo, steppin fetching**, and let us not forget the N word. Verse 43 the stranger that is within thee shall get up above thee very high and thou shall come down very low. Think for a moment who owns the businesses in the black community? **The Asians sell our women their hair, the Spanish sell us our fruits and vegetables, the Arabs sell us our liquor, the Indians/Pakistanians sell us our gasoline**. All of the vendors that come to our neighborhood and sell to us look like somebody else. The money that they make in our neighborhood they take back and deposit in their bank. This is what the scripture means when it says the stranger shall get very high and you shall be low. Verse 44 he shall lend to thee and thou shalt not lend to him he shall be the head and thou shalt be the tail. This can't be pointing to the white Jew because he is the banker of this generation and he does all of the lending. The so called Negro does all the borrowing. Verse 46 and they (curses) shall be upon thee for a sign and for a wonder and upon thy seed forever. You see when you saw all of these signs you were supposed to wake up to consciousness, to self to say hey ,that looks like me! You never read this because your Minister told you that you are a New Testament Christian, so you never examined the writings of the prophets. See Isaiah 42: 22 this is a people robbed and spoiled they are all of them snared in holes and **they are hid in prison houses. Though the Negro in America makes up 12% of the population**

he represents 50% of the inmates that are incarcerated in this country and again the words of this book point to you and only you! Isaiah 42: verse 24 who gave Jacob for a spoil and Israel to the robbers (white man) did not the Lord he against whom we have sinned? For they would not walk in his ways neither were they obedient unto his law! Verse 25 **therefore he hath poured upon him the fury of his anger and the strength** of battle and it hath set him on fire round about yet he knew not and it burned him **yet he laid it not to heart**. This was family business between us and our God and the strange thing is the Lord said thru the prophet Isaiah," It never came to your mind (heart) that all of the things that befell you Mr. Negro was from my hand. This quarrel was and is a family dispute between the God of Israel and his people that just happened played out in front of the global community. What he did to us was a warning to the rest of the world that if I do this to my people that are called by my name you need to beware of me! See Leviticus 26: 15-46, verse 21 and if you walk contrary unto me and will not hearken unto me I will bring seven times more plagues upon you according to your sin. Verse 23 and if you will not be reformed by me by these things but will walk contrary unto me verse 24 then will I also walk contrary unto you and will punish you yet seven times for your sins verse 25 and **I will send a sword upon you that shall avenge the**

quarrel of my covenant. Ladies and gentlemen this is why the so called Negro is in the economic, social, and mental condition that he finds himself in, no matter where you find him. This is the reason that we were spread out among all the nations on earth because of this family dispute between us and our God! What is God's bone of contention with the black Hebrew Israelite? We refuse to keep his commandments and to walk in his statues, we worship the gods of the nations around about us! And so we were delivered into the hands of our enemies. See Leviticus 26: verse 17 and I will set my face against you and ....they that hate you shall reign over you and you shall flee when none pursues you, verse 33 and I will scatter you among the heathen. The one who calls himself a Jew isn't scattered among the nations because there are some nations in Arabia that would kill him on sight! Make no mistake about it. This is a historical known fact that the British are descendents of the barbarians of Europe and were and are the most heathenistic! The white man hates us why? One, because I'm convinced that he has known since Morton Stanleys picture of the Ashanti priest crossing the Prah river in Niger back in 1848 that the Negro is Israel and two because the white man has a huge secret and I shall tell it to you before I end this book.

THE LYNCHING OF UNARMED MEN WOMEN AND CHILDREN

This was the time that the Lord talked about when he said your life would hang in doubt. The **Tuskegee Institute recorded 3446 lynchings** in the south between the years 1882 and 1968. Nearly 200 lynching bills were introduced into Congress but only 3 passed the House, seven Presidents between 1890 and 1952 petitioned Congress to pass a federal law. It couldn't get

CURSED IS HE THAT HANGETH ON A TREE

past the Senate. This was the mental condition of the whites in America and this is what our father's had to deal with. Think about it after 246 years of free labor the Negro should have been loved by these Southern whites but that would not be the case. I guess they must have missed the free labor, or being able to rape or kill other human beings of color, or pillage steal and squat on other nation's lands. Maybe it was the fact that they had to get up off their lazy kidnapping asses and do some real work of their own for a change that prompted this hatred toward a man that could now search out his own devices and reconstruct his family first and then his past.

JIM CROW LAWS 1876-1965

These laws provided for the segregation of public places, bathrooms, restaurants, public schools, drinking fountains, and before I forget the Military! While writing this book I have begun to realize that the white church in America failed God, for if this institution had stood on the side of righteousness the criminal institution of slavery could never have gained a footing on American soil. I must note the fact that under segregation the Negro owned his own businesses, the Negro professional baseball league, his own Black Wall street, and he received an education from those who loved him! He was taught to love himself, when people love you they point out the error of your ways, they tell you what not to do to succeed in life. This was the type of mentoring and tutoring that we received from the segregated black schools that we ran. The black child was taught the truth about his former glory.

CURSED IN THE FIELD AND CURSED IN THE CITY

DEUTERONOMY 28:16

No matter where Israel went in this country **the quarrel of the covenant** followed him, the curses that would be on you for a sign followed him from the country to the city. Notice God says he was slightly displeased but the heathen helped further the affliction, meaning they went to far! At about this time the white man in America had just about rolled back the clock on any gains this Negro had acheieved since 1865 and he had his foot so far up the Negros' behind that he probably thought he had grown another leg. But again the God of Israel heard the moanings and groanings of his people Israel in America and he raised us up saviors. This section right here is for all of you zealots and fanatics in America, some of you have been led to believe that if a brother or sister has not come into the knowledge of self that he is to be shown disdain and contempt. That brother of sister is still the inheritance of the Lord and don't you forget it. In the process of time the Lord will open up his or her eyes just like he did yours and mine. Remember that you once also was blind and now you see. this was not by any act of your own but by the mercy of a loving God.

CHAPTER 7   IF IT BE A SON THEN KILL HIM

See Nehemiah 9:26 nevertheless they were disobedient and rebelled against thee and cast thy law behind their backs and slew thy prophets which testified against them to turn them to thee and they wrought great provocations. Verse 27 therefore thou deliveredst them into the hands of their enemies who vexed them and in the time of their trouble when they cried unto thee thou heardest them from heaven and according to thy manifold mercies **thou gavest them saviours** who saved them out of the hand of their enemies! Once again the living God intervened on our behalf when he sent us Martin Luther King. I must put this in here because the Lord is not limited in his power, he can deliver with a blind man or a seeing man, a Hebrew or a Muslim, a Christian or a Buddist. The Lord can use a wicked man or a righteous man, there really is no searching out his ways but the fact is he can deliver. If a man is drowning will he care if the object that saves him is a tree vine or a floating log? Will he care if his deliverance came by way of a Jew or a Muslim, I say nay! His only saying will be thank God! I would like to examine two saviours of the Negro race Martin Luther King and Malcom X.

RARE IMAGE OF MARTIN AND MALCOM X

The most high brought Martin Luther King along at a time when the heads of all the black men in America stooped for shame. History talks about the march on Washington, white people hadn't seen that many Hebrews in one place in their entire life. Martin will be remembered for the Rosa Parks Montgomery bus incident 1955, where this mother in Israel uttered those famous words that echoed around the globe," **NO!** No, I refuse to get up out of my seat and move to the back of the bus! "The garbage strikes, the Birmingham protests against segregation, the Nobel Peace Prize but you know something, to me that was pale in comparison for what he did for the black men and women of his generation. Martin showed the brothers and sisters (we) together can turn the world upside down and they did! A very interesting fact about Martin Luther King was that he and Malcom had come to an understanding of working together for the sake of the Negro nation. In fact few people are aware that Martin Luther King had started to form his own party to run for the Presidency of the United States. In 1967 William F. Pepper suggested to King that he should challenge Lyndon B. Johnson for the Democratic Party nomination but King refused instead opting to form his own party. The National Conference for New Politics (NCNP). This was the platform he would use for a presidential run with Dr. Benjamin Spock as his Vice President.

THE BODY OF MARTIN LUTHER BEING DRAWN BY A MULE

AND PHAROAH SAID" IF IT BE A SON KILL HIM"

What did Pharoah say? Exodus 1: verse 15 and the king of Egypt spake to the Hebrew midwives of which the name of the one was Shiph-rah and the name of the other Pu'ah verse 16 and he said, when you do the office of a midwife the to the Hebrew women and see them upon the stools **if it be a son then you shall kill him** but if it be a daughter then she shall live! This was the attitude of Pharoahs generation, it was the attitude of the whites in Martin Luther King's generation and this is attitude of this current white American generation. Take notice the racist whites **didn't**

assassinate Coretta did they? Because the commandment is still the same, let the black woman live, but kill the black men. What happened to Martin was genocide. Let's examine the United Nation definition of genocide.

Genocide

Article II: In the present Convention, genocide means any of the following acts committed with intent to destroy, in whole or in part, a national, ethnical, racial or religious group, as such:

(a) Killing members of the group;
(b) Causing serious bodily or mental harm to members of the group;
(c) Deliberately inflicting on the group conditions of life calculated to bring about its physical destruction in whole or in part;
(d) Imposing measures intended to prevent births within the group;
(e) Forcibly transferring children of the group to another group.

Article III: The following acts shall be punishable:

(a) Genocide;
(b) Conspiracy to commit genocide;
(c) Direct and public incitement to commit genocide;
(d) Attempt to commit genocide;
(e) Complicity in genocide. "

Looking backwards from our present vantage point we can see that what the United States did to brother Martin comes under the United Nations charter as Genocide, but what about the number of brothers who have been shot down by racist white cops, electrocuted (Tasered) legally on the streets of this country or even murdered on death row while being innocent. Is this too not genocide? What about the savage organization in all the poor Negro communities called Planned Parenthood? Examine this statistic 550,000 black babies are aborted in the womb each year in the United States and over the last 30 years that would correspond to 15 million of our children aborted by Planned Parenthood! Is this not imposing measures to prevent births in a group, the black community? Rest in peace elder King we will see you in the resurrection and you will indeed wear the crown of a King, peace!

THE BODY OF MALCOM X BEING DRAWN BY NY POLICE

AND PHAROAH SAID" IF IT BE A SON KILL HIM

Any student of so called African American history knows the story of Malcom Little, or Malcom X, he started life as a street hustler,he eventually went to prison where he learned how to read and write. He joined the Nation of Islam and became an activist, that's right, he fought for the real freedom of the Hebrew Israelite in America. Malcom represented the military side of our conflict in America. He was intelligent and articulate but most of all the man was fearless. His thing was nationhood for the Negro because this man understood from the historical record that we are the seed of the empire. I used to get a rush about our fathers in Africa building 53 nations now 54, but after I read the account of the **Ashanti empire** I began to understand what this seed is capable of. The white historians in this captivity know that what I write is free of lies, and again Malcolm's **wife and daughter went unharmed** because it is written **if it's a daughter you shall save it alive!** The commandment if it be a son kill him is not relegated to just the black man. What I''ve noticed throughout history is that any whiteman that will try to help this captive negro shall also be killed. Case in point **John F. Kennedy, John Brown and Robert Kennedy.** Two Governors in the state of Illinois have been incarcerated for helping black people , Governor Thompson and Blogaoavich. Governor Thompson did away with the death penalty when he saw all of the innocent black men being electrocuted on death row over crimes they did not commit, for this he was rewarded with a jail cell. Rest in peace General Malcom , we remember your sacrifice and you are loved!

MEDGAR EDGARS

AND PHARAOH SAID IF IT BE A SON KILL HIM

There is no way that I could leave out this brother from Alcorn State who gave his life in registering voters in the South. Medgar Edgars was an N.A.A.C.P activist who gave his life for his people. The white KKK member, Byron De La Beckwith who murdered Medgar in 1963 was acquitted by two all white juries in the State of Mississippi. This murderer was not convicted until 30 years later! The edict of Pharaoh still held sway if it be a son kill him , so again the woman and children were spared!

CHAPTER 8 THE UNTHINKABLE

The Lord says that if he didn't intervene then the enemy would vaunt himself and say the Lord has not done this, to these black Hebrew Israelites I did this to them. See Deuteronomy 32:26 and I said, **I would scatter them into corners**, I would make **the remembrance of them to cease from among men** verse 27 were it not that I feared the wrath of **the enemy**, lest their adversaries should **behave themselves strangely**, and lest **they should say our hand is high and the Lord has not done all of this!** As a result of the quarrel of the covenant the so called Negro finds himself in the hands of those that hate him, (Europeans) it was necessary for the Lord to scatter the black Israelite into all the nations under the sun.

History records that we were the greatest fighting men the world had ever seen, feared among nations. See Deuteronomy 32: how should **one chase a thousand and two put ten thousand to flight**, this is one of the reasons I knew that the hand of the Lord was against us, there is no way these Europeans could enslave us and maintain this type of control over us unless our God had permitted it! It appears that in our times of hardship the Lord raises up one of the brothers to sit on the throne of our enemies he did it in the times when Joseph and the patriarchs were down in Egypt. The most high raised Joseph out of prison and made him ruler next to Pharaoh. See Genesis 41:38 and Pharaoh said unto his servants, can we find such a one as this is, a man in whom the spirit of God is? Verse 39 and pharaoh said unto Joseph verse 40 you shall be over my house and according unto thy word shall all my people be ruled only in the throne will I be greater than you. This is an image of Joseph that was found on a coin in the land of Egypt, as you can see he is a black Hebrew Israelite, and according to the article the back of the coin had images of wheat and corn and named Joseph Viceroy of Egypt. **If you take this image of Joseph and match it with the pictures that came out of the tomb of Ben Hassan (courtesy of the History Channel) in Egypt it** is a perfect fit, he looks just like the rest of the brothers and sisters whose images were on the wall of the tomb.

BLACK HEBREW ISRAELITE MEN

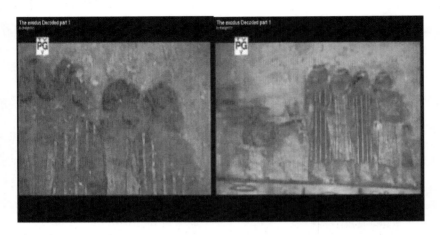

JOSEPH OF THE BIBLE

Verse 41 and Pharaoh said unto Joseph see I have set thee over all the land of Egypt. Verse 42 and Pharaoh took off his ring from his hand and put it upon Josephs' hand and arrayed him in vestures of fine linen and put a gold chain about his neck. Genesis 41: verse 43 and pharaoh made Joseph to ride it the second chariot which he had and they cried before him **Bow the knee** and he made him ruler over all the land of Egypt. The real historians (if there are any left) of this modern age know indeed that one of our fathers ruled over one of the most magnificent and splendid world powers of any generation, the kingdom of the Pharaohs. History also shows that **Otto I or Otto the Great the Holy Roman Emperor, ruler over the Holy Roman Empire and his wife are depicted as black people.**

OTTO THE GREAT

Edith of England and Otto I, Holy Roman Emperor - Married in 929 A.D.

Go back and read your history books, Otto the great ruled the whole entire Earth! Examine this next image of Severus the first black Roman Emperor.

SERVERUS BLACK ROMAN EMPEROR
193A.D-211A.D

Now the history of black Septimius is interesting because those who enslaved us, the (English or British) have it in their archives that we ruled England as the King and from England the Negro ruled the Holy Roman Empire! Known as Septimius Serverus, a North African Libyan who ruled the Holy Roman Empire around193 A.D. Toward the end of the book I will reveal the secret of the European. In my lifetime, I witnessed the running for the presidency of the United States by Jesse Jackson in 1984 a black man. At that time, based on

JESSE JACKSON

what had been taught to me by my white professors and my ignorant black professors I thought that these events were the first of its kind. You can't kick against Jesse, his record in the human rights arena speaks for itself. In 1983, he cabled Assad directly to plead for the release of downed pilot Robert Goodman Jr. When Assad failed to respond, Jackson flew to Damascus and worked his way through a tangle of lower-level Syrian bureaucrats before securing a meeting with the Syrian leader. (The success of that mission jump started Jackson's 1984 Presidential campaign.) He had hostages released in Cuba, Iraq, and Yugoslavia. His Operation Bread Basket, the boycotts, we watched history in the making but he would not achieve the goal of being king. The crown was reserved for one Barrack Obama. It's interesting to note how these Europeans have portrayed the election of the first black president in the United States as some sort of phenomenon, but if you didn't have the people would have you to believe that this was the first

time in human historical records, you wouldn't know. These history that **a black man ruled over a white nation, let alone a white empire**. This is the reason it is important that these Negro historians who have been taught a curriculum at these white institutions' and the racist white historians do some real research and tell, not just black people the truth, but tell the truth to the white youth! So far the legacy of Barrack Obama is still being written but I will go on record to say that to hold the title of the most powerful man in the world and to be treated the way he has by this racist white media is mindboggling.

CHAPTER 9   THE MORNING TRAIN

The so called Negro has been away from his home and his land for 392 years if you count from 1619 the year the first captive came into the Virginian colony. For the history purist reading this book it would be 2722 years away from home for the 10 tribes and 2000 years away from home for Benjamin, Judah, and Levi. That being said, I would like to put a question to you. Can you tell me if you have read anywhere in the scriptures or any history book concerning the captivity of the Negro Hebrew Israelite. Who told the Negro that his sojourning in the land of the Indians would last forever? The God of Israel set a time limit on the outcasts of Israel and **believe it or not our sojourning in North America is tied into the time that God has set for the Europeans to rule the earth**. These are ancient things that I am about to speak about, the Lord set the bounds of human civilization in the writings of the Prophet Moses. In Leviticus 23rd chapter verse 3, 6 days shall work be done but the seventh day is the Sabbath of rest a holy convocation ye shall do no work therein it Sabbath of the Lord in all your dwellings. This is the first clue, the Lord told Moses that this man has 6 days to work, is God talking about mans days or what? We'll have to travel back to the very beginning and ear hustle on a conversation that God is having with Adam about the concept of a day. See Genesis 2:15-16 verse 16 and the Lord God commanded the man saying of every tree of the garden thou may freely eat verse 17 but of the tree of the knowledge of good and evil thou shall not eat of it **for in the day that thou eat thereof thou shall surely die.** So now we have to see how many years make up one of Gods days. Lets' go to 2nd Peter 3: 8 verse 8 but beloved be not ignorant of this one thing that one day with the Lord is 1000 years and a thousand years one day. King David wrote in Psalm 90: 4 That a thousand years in thy sight are but as yesterday when it is past and as a watch in the night. All of this sounds good but can it be proven out? Let's see how long the old timers lived. Let's see if any one of them made it to 1000 years. Go with me to Genesis 5:5 and all the days of Adam **was 930 years** and he died, Genesis 5: 8 and **all the days of Seth was 912 years** and he died Genesis 5:11 and **all the days of Enos were 905 years** and he died, Genesis 5:14 and **all the days of Cainan were 910 years** and he died, Genesis 5:17 and **all the days of Mahalaleel was 895 years** and he died, Genesis 5: 20 and **all the days of Jared were 962 years** and he died, Genesis 5: 27 and **all the days of Methusalah were 969 years** and he died, Genesis 9: 29 and **all the days of Noah was 950 years** and he died. As you can see none of the old timers lived an entire day or one of God's days which happens to be 1000 years. So when God gave man 6 days to work he really gave him 6000 years to govern the planet. The second part of this equation is how many years have elapsed of these 6000 years?

CALCULATION FOR 6000 YEARS

COLUMN –A	COLUMN-B	COLUMN-C
FROM THE CREATION OF ADAM 4000 B.C	TO THE THE MURDER OF JESUS CHRIST 29 1/2 A.D	4000 YEARS
	JESUS DIED ON THE CROSS	
FROM THE MURDER OF JESUS CHRIST	TO THE YEAR 2011 A.D	2000 YEARS
		6000 YEARS

As you can see from the spreadsheet that I have prepared for you that I count the 6000 years of human history from the time that Adam was created (COLUMN-A) to the murder of Jesus Christ 4000 years and from the murder of Christ to this current generation 2000 years giving me a total of 6000 years of human history or 6 of Gods' days. Is there any proof on the earth concerning this supposed hypothesis? Of course there is, for starters this man only has 6000 years of written history, the oldest writtings that have been found are the cuneiform tablets located in Mesopotamia.

IMAGE OF A CUNEIFORM TABLET

What these archaeologists are unearthing are the writings of the black headed ones of Shinar (sumer),

ELAM   **GUDEA**   **SHULGI**   **SARGON**

These are the black Mesopotamians that the historians have written about so pointedly stating that they are black but not the sons of Ham! Of interest is the fact that the black men of Mesopotamia were credited with inventing **math**, the **wheel**, the **sexagesamal system**, **astronomy** and **writing**, the **first medicine book** was found in Mesopotamia, In fact the first known language is credited to these black men. This may be the reason the European historians have been lying all these years, saying that Africa is the cradle of civilization, when in fact Mesopotamia is the cradle of civilization. They did not want you to know that Adam, Seth, Cainan, Enos, Mahalaeel, Methusalah, Enoch, Lamech, Jared and Noah were all black Mesopotamian men!

In the book of Genesis God said that he put Adam and Eve near the Tigris and Euphrates river. Ladies and gentleman the Tigris and Euphrates runs thru Mesopotamia. The archaeologists say the oldest bones was found in Africa, I have no problem with that, people go for walks all the time, the person originated in Mesopotamian and walked westward into Africa. Let God be true and every man a liar. The Sumerians used a reed (like a drinking straw) to draw web shaped images in clay, then they would either bake the clay or allow them to dry in the sun. You have been taught all of your life that Egypt was the oldest civilization, and this is a lie. The oldest civilization on earth was **Adam's civilization** and it was located in **Mesopotamia, the land of the black headed ones,** which would mean that Adam (interpreted red clay) was a black man. These archaeologist aren't stupid, these people are just sick! You mean to tell me that everybody in Mesopotamia was black except Adam, that everybody in Mesopotamia was black except Abraham and that everybody in Mesopotamia was black except Shem? Stop with the foolishness, we have had about as much of the malarkey that we can stand! The cradle of civilization was in Mesopotamia and not in Africa. The next piece of evidence that I will present to support a 6000 year human history is some of the oldest trees found on earth.

METHUSALAH	SARV E ABARKOOH

4800 YR OLD PINE	**4000 YR OLD CYPRESS**

The oldest tree found on earth is the Great Basin Bristle Cone Pine at 4800 years, the method of dating trees is simple, each tree ring inside the tree represents 1 year of the trees existance. Now some of you are thinking the earth has to be over 6000 years old because the oldest rock found on earth was dated at 4.2 billion years. I have no problem with the age of the earth because the Bible says that in the beginning God created the heaven and the earth, which would imply that there is no way to put a date on the beginning. And in the 2nd chapter of Genesis the Lord talks about the generations of the heavens and the earth, this would suggest that the earth has went thru cycles. The point that I'm trying to make is simple the scientists and archaeologists know for a fact that they only have 6000 years of written human history. Prehistoric man is a fabrication of the white mans mind, this is his way of shoving his evolution garbage down mankinds throat.

Prehistoric man, the time that man recorded nothing, if you believe this I got a lake for sale. Even little girls that play hopscotch will draw on the ground and what about the graffetti artis? This man is inclined to draw and write, as witnessed by the cuneiform tablets. The black kings of Mesopotamia and the black kings of Egypt ruled the earth for the first 3400 years of mans existence on earth, this is fact not fiction. The white historians know this is fact because you didn't get white rulership over the entire earth until 606 B.C with the arrival of Nebuchadnezzar of Babylon. Now Jesus the Christ made a statement in the book of Luke the 21st chapter verse 24 talking about the invasion of Jerusalem by the Romans, it reads, and they shall fall by the edge of the sword and shall be led away captive into all nations and Jerusalem shall be trodden down of the Gentiles **until the times of the gentiles be fulfilled.** I got news for you **white colonizing, globilizing, enslaving, resource stealing, nation invading,** white powers. The Lord set a time when white rulership would end and on paper that time occurred in 2004, so right now you are ruling on the Lords day. See Isaiah 60:19,22 the sun shall be no more thy light by day neither for brightness shall the moon give light unto thee but the Lord shall be unto thee an everlasting light and thy God thy glory. Verse 22 a little one shall become a thousand and a small one a strong nation **I the**

Lord will hasten it in his time. You'll need to read the entire 60th chapter of Isaiah to get some understanding, this is referring to the second coming of Christ and I know it to be fact because he talks about Israel coming back into the land and the sun not shining. This will only happen in the day of the Lord. The Gentiles (white nations) rulership will end when black Jesus shows up with the angels and the saints. See Joel the 3rd chapter you'll need to read the entire chapter to see that it's talking about the gathering of Israel but verse 9 reads, **proclaim you this among the Gentiles prepare war** wake up the mighty men let all the men of war draw near let them come up verse 10 beat your plowshares into swords and your purnninghooks into spears let the weak say I am strong. Verse 11 **assemble yourselves** and come all ye heathen and gather yourselves together round abouth thither cause thy mighty ones to come down o Lord. Why is the proclamation aimed at the Gentiles? Because it is written in Matthew 24: 21,22 verse 22 and **if those days had not been shortened no flesh would be saved**, in order for the earth to be freed from the grip of these evil white nations God must put down their rulership. Also who possesses the weapons of mass destruction on this earth? The white nations: **United States, Russia , United Kingdom , China, France, and Pakistan**, All of these nations are Gentile nations. In case you haven't noticed, black Hebrews are spread among all the nations of the world but in order for the Lord to free his people he must go to war with the white powers. The white powers of the earth and her allies will try to go to war with the eternal. This is what Armagadden is all about plus this white man dosen't want to relinquish his grip on the poor of this world. When God shows up the foolish white nations will attempt to hold on to the thing that God loves the most and that is the Hebrew Israelite. God destroyed Egypt because she had the love of God in her bosom. The European powers have destroyed themselves with their treatment of the sons of God over the last 2700 years. The white man will attempt to kill God. They think because he allowed himself to be crucified on the cross 2000 years ago that it can be done again. See Psalm 2:1-4 verse 1 why do the heathen rage and the people imagine a vain thing? Verse 2 the kings of the earth set themselves and the rulers take council toether against the Lord and against his anointed, verse 3 saying let us break their bands asunder and cast away their cords fro us verse 4 He that sitteth in the heavens shall laugh the Lord shall have them in derision. For all of you who have it in your mind to volunteer for the armed forces **beware that you don't fight against our God and our King**, because if you do you will receive the reward of the wicked, let me show you. In the book of Zachariah the 14th chapter and the 12th

verse and this shall be the plague wherewith the Lord will smite all the people that have fought against Jerusalem **their flesh shall consume away while they stand upon their feet and their eyes shall consume away in their holes and their tongue shall consume away in their mouth.** Do we have anything in the history of this man that I could use as a visual aid so you can get an idea what God is going to do to this rebellious man? Yes unfortunately I do, history has recorded images of this cruel white man dropping the atomic bomb on the citizens of Japan, Nagasakki and Hiroshima, and this is what war with Jesus the Christ will look like! For all of you Christians who go to church every Sunday and hear about Jesus being a cuddly fuzzy guy it is true. Unfortunately just like we all have a button that if you push it you will see that other side of us. Our God has another side to himself that he dosen't like to display, case in point the flood and the lake of fire looming in the future for the wicked.

CHAPTER 10 WAR WITH THE GOD OF ISRAEL

See Revelation 19:11-14 and I saw heaven opened and behold a white horse and he that sat upon him was called faithful and true and in righteousness he doth judge and make war. verse 12 **his eyes were as a flame of fire**, Revelation 1:14,15 **his hair was like lambs wool, his feet as if burned in a furnace**. Revelation 19: 13 he was clothed with a vesture dipped in blood and **his name is called the word of God** and the armies which were in heaven followed him upon white horses clothed in fine linen white and clean verse 15 and out of his mouth goeth a sharp sword that with it he should smite the nations; and he shall rule them with a rod of iron.

IMAGE FROM TURKISH MONASTERY 1300 A.D

The Sümela Monastery, Turkey - circa 1,300 A.D.

IMAGE FROM TURKISH MONASTERY 1300 A.D

The Sümela Monastery, Turkey - circa 1,300 A.D.

THE 2ND COMING OF THE BLACK JESUS CHRIST

The United States detonated a nuclear bomb on Hiroshma and Nagasaka in World War II, the heat of the blast was so intense that some of the people were vaporized where they sat. This is what NATO, EUROPEAN UNION, RUSSIA, CHINA and her allies have waiting on them in this future conflict with Jesus.

THE AFTER AFFECTS OF THE ATOM BOMB:

VAPORIZED LIVING SOUL

VAPORIZED **REDUCED TO ASHES**

MOTHER AND CHILD BURNED TO DEATH

I am from the hood and we have a thing in the hood called a drive by, that's where somebody drives down the street in a raggedy car shooting out the windows at someone that they have a problem with. Usually these guys shoot the innocent bystander and that is what will happen to anyone that gets in the Lord's way! The shadow on the bus stop and the shadow on the steps is all that was left of two functioning human beings! You don't want any of this do you?

THE CITIES OF THE WORLD

What about the Europeans beautiful cities? See Revelation 16:19 and **the cities of the nations fell**. I want you to see the destruction that the bomb left in its wake on the cities of Japan and the destruction of German cities in its wars.

HIROSHIMA DESTROYED

THE DESTRUCTION OF COLOGNE GERMANY

THE DESTRUCTION OF HAMBURG GERMANY

MASS GRAVES OF HIROSHIMA

If you are reading this book you are blessed because you are getting a sneak preview into the 2nd coming of Jesus the Christ. The destruction of the Gentiles (white European powers) coincides with the returning of the Hebrew Israelite (so called Negro) back to Jerusalem. It also means the the native **Indians will get their lands back, the aborigines of Australia will get their land back, the South Africans will get their lands back from the Dutch and the true Egyptian will get his land back from the Arabs**. I want to make this very clear the liberation of the so called Negro is actually the liberation of the entire planet.

It also means that these Europeans' in America have to go back to Europe where they originated from. So as you can see the Lord never told the black man that he would be in the land of captivity forever and the liberation of the black man will coincide with the destruction of the white power system as we know it. How will the world receive the news of the European demise? See Ezekiel 35: 14 **the whole earth shall rejoice**! The entire planet shall rejoice at the fall of the white international banking cartel, and the white colonizers, NATO, and THE EUROPEAN UNION.

THE EVERYMAN PROPHECY

In the book of **Leviticus the 25th chapter** verse 8: and thou shalt number seven sabbaths of years unto thee seven times seven years and the space of the seven sabbths of years shall be unto thee forty and nine years ,verse 9 then shalt thou cause the trumpet of the jubile to sound on the tenth day of the seventh month in the day of atonement **shall you make the trumpet sound** throughout all your land verse 10 and you shall hallow the fiftheth year and proclaim liberty throughout all the land unto all the inhabitants thereof **it shall be a jubile unto and you shall return every man unto his possession and you shall return <u>every man unto his family</u>**! Verse 13 In the year of jubile you shall return every man unto his possession. Now check this out, when that trumpet blows in the year of jubilee **every man, not some men, but every man must go back to his family and his land**, the socalled Negro (Hebrew Israelite) is part of **the every man prophecy**, every man including the Negro in America must return to the land of his fathers whether he wants to or not! See **Isaiah 13:10** for the stars of heaven and the constellations thereof shall not give their light **the sun shall be darkened** in his going forth and the moon shall not cause her light to shine, why? Verse 14 because <u>**every man (Negro) shall turn to his own people** and flee **every one into his own land**</u>. You see every man was given a plot of land when the Lord divided to the nations their inheritance in the days of Peleg around 2243B.C, I know you have been intoxicated by this Europeans' technology, but believe me when the Lord comes back, the European will flee from you while attempting to flee from Christ. In the book of Revelation 11:15 it talks about a 7th trumpet being blown and when this trumpet is blown the kingdoms of this world have become the kingdoms of our Christ, the angel of the Lord is referring to this white power structure on the earth right now. If you notice **the former white colonizing nations and white enslaving nations are to this day attacking nations of color. France, United States , England, and Dutch**, all of these nations have hidden themselves in world organizations with names like **NATO, European Union or the Allies.** These nations have not changed. Instead of colonizing nations of color they send in the International bankers under the pretense of helping the black nation. The International Monetary Fund and the World Bank operate under the umbrella of globalization and free market. This is how it works, these banks give loans to nations with strings attached like, get rid of your President, interest that can never be paid back, sell off your private government controlled industries to outside investors, allow the G8 nations to flood your markets with goods sold lower than your markets and after you've sold the people out , the new dictator or President flees the country with billions. What are the people left with? Recession and depression in that order, then chaos sets in and these same white nations, under the disguise of the United Nations, send in troops to restore order. Now not only is your country owned by outside investors but you also find yourself occupied! This is what happened to 53 nations in Africa after post colonialism, and unto this day the continent has not repaid back the interest on these loans. This is why the Bible teaches that usury (INTEREST) is a moral crime! It is secret bondage to the lender , they know for a fact that you can never pay the interest back, let alone the principal. Examine America's debt, 90% of her debt is the interest that she is being charged by the Federal

Reserve to print money for us. The point that I am trying to make is simple. The only one who can destroy this good old boy power structure is the Creator.

CHAPTER 11 THE ANSWER TO THE NEGRO QUESTION

Based on **the images taken from the tombs , D.N.A, artifacts, the Bible, and the secret air lifts of Ethiopian Jews, the Negro is none other than the original Jew**. The **law of darkness** was used exclusively against us so that by not reading and doing our own studies we would never come to the knowledge of self. The second question that was raised was his origination, the so called Negro in America did not originate in Africa but had his origination in Mesopotamia, the land of the black headed people. Our father Abraham crossed over from Mesopotamia (the meaning of the word Hebrew) into Canaan and there our fathers were born, Issac and Jacob. From Jacobs loins came the 12 tribes and from his 12 sons the whole of Israel. We had colonies in Alexandria, Carthage, Cyrene and Elephantine, the black Jewish colonies descended into Africa during times of invasions such as the Assyrian invasion of 722 B.C, the Babyloinan invasion 609 Based on **the images taken from the tombs , D.N.A,** B.C , the Roman destruction of Jerusalem in 70A.D, the Arab invasion in 640 A.D and the destruction of Jerusalem by Hadrian 132 A.D. It was from these invasions that our fathers situated themselves along the wheat coast, gold coast and slave coasts of Africa and from here our fathers formed one of the greatest black empires that the west fails to teach black children about, the Ashanti Empire. Now I shall proceed to trace the Negros lineage from Shem, Luke 3: 23-38, verse 36 which was the son of **Arphaxad**, which was the son of **Shem** verse 38 which was the son of **Enos**, which was the son of **Seth**, which was the son of **Adam, which was the son of God**! The Negro in America is the true son of God for we trace our lineage thru Shem, not Ham nor Japheth and this has been proven! The title of the book is the Negro question , who is he and where is he from. I have attempted to prove to you that the so called Negro in America has his orgins in Mesopotamia and in that region of the world were black people. It has been shown that our fathers migrated from Mesopotamia South into Africa, beginning with Abraham, where he looked like his brother Ham. **In fact, when the Lord became upset with our fathers he deported them not to Africa but he sent them packing back to Mesopotamia from whence they came. First to Assyria of Mesopotamia and secondly to Babylon which was in Mesopotamia**. The migration of the black Mesopotamian into Africa is no more a freakish event than the barbarians of Europe migrating from Northern Europe to Southern Europe in the 5th century. What then is the solution to the Negro question?

The solution to the Negro question is simple, the Europeans in America will never respect the achievements of black Americans they have proven that with their treatment of the Negro President Obama. The Negro has proven his worth to this country, we made them rich, we fought in all of his wars; Civil War, Spanish American War, Mexican War, WW1,WW2, Grenada, Vietnam , Iraq, Indian wars, Korean War, Gulf War, and Afghanastan. America's enemies were our enemies even though we have been treated like the dung that the dog leaves in the grass. From the year 1865 to 2011, in 146 years, we have caught up to the white American in education, technology, sciences, politics, athletics, but what can we achieve after such a sprint on the universal time line? **The only thing left for this Negro to accomplish is the end game, and that being the formulation of his own nation**. There were 193 nations represented at the United Nations, and there were 162 nations represented that didn't have individually the population that the Negro in America has and that being **42,000,000 souls**. We have all the skill sets of nationhood, a black President , black generals, scientists, morticians, educators, businessmen and asstronauts. It is time for the Negro in America to be seated at the table of nations, this is the final solution. The white establishment knows that what I write is truth because all white people have one thing in common. White people want to maintain white rulership they just differ on the ways to do it. Case in point the Klu Klux Klan vs the Democratic Party or the Tea Part vs the Republican Party. You black folk had thoughts of nostalgia when Obama got elected but guess what? Nothing has changed and what further proof do you need that you need your own nation.

CHAPTER 12 THE WHITE JEWISH QUESTION

I found it quite amusing as I had to gather all of the information that I showed you to prove that the Negro in America is the Hebrew Israelite of the Bible. I showed you the replica of the Ark of the Covenant carbon dated between 700 and 1000 years old, I showed you the images of the black Jews from the tomb of Ben Hassan, I showed you the different airlifts into Jerusalem of the black Ethiopian Jews, I showed you the Sambatyan Jews of Nigeria, I showed you the London Times article of the Ashanti priest crossing the Prah river with Holy to Yhwh on his cap and the breastplate, I showed you the coin with Josephs image on it , I showed you the image of Hagab the Judean archer, I recalled your attention to the letter the

Queen of the Ashanti wrote to the Queen of England about how the Ashanti worshipped the God of the Sabbath, and I showed you how the Ashanti got there name, that these were the people of Ashan in the bible. **What about the white Jew in Jerusalem? Where is his proof of origination, where are his artifacts, and what exactley did he present to the United Nations in 1948 that they gave him a charter for nationhood and the land of our fathers?** In order to answer that question we must answer **the white Jewish question**, in a very deliberate and forensic science type of manner. The white Jewish question begins with a trip backwards in time to a small nation situated near the Black Sea and Caspian Sea in Europe called the Khazars. **The King of the Khazars traces his lineage not thru Shem but thru Japheth** the son of Noah. A letter is written from King Joseph of the Khazars in which he details his people's lineage, " we have found in the family registers of our fathers , Joseph asserts boldly that **Togarma,** the son of Japheth(Gentiles) had ten sons and the names of their offspring are as follows: **Uigur, Dursu, Avars, Huns, Basilii, Tarniakh, Khazars, Zagora, Bulgars, Sabir <u>we are the sons of Khazars the seventh</u>! This is an official document from the now deceased Khazar nation stating to the world we are not from Shem but we converted to Judaism as sons of Japheth**! See The 13th tribe Koestler page 72, these people kept the Russians (vikings) from invading Arabia and kept the Arabs from invading Europe! The Khazars were a Turkish kingdom that was situated between the Black Sea and the Caspian Sea. The Khazar settlement is mentioned in the Crimea, the Ukraine, Hungary, Poland and Lithuain and these settlements migrated into Russia and Poland.

MAP SHOWING LOCATION OF KHAZARS

Listen this section of the book is not meant in any form or fashion to produce hate, racism or bias against the white Jews of Israel. I am simply trying to answer the Jewish question that has become a burning fire in the circles of the wise men! Based on historical correspondance between the Muslim Caliphs and the King of Kharzaria it has come to light that the Khazars chose Judaism over Islam and Christianity so as not to be a servant to the Pope or the Caliph. Historically, the people of Khazaria were a Turkish Finnish people that originated in Asia that entered Europe by land route north of the Caspian Sea. It has been recorded that they settled in eastern Europe and established the Khazar Kingdom. The Khazar King, Joseph, chose Judaism as the state religion. The Khazar Kingdom collected tribute from at least 25 nations that they conquered and from these 25 nations the Khazar King reportedly by force or consent married one of their daughters so he had at least 25 wives. It is interesting to note that this kingdom lasted for 500 years, yet it is as if these people who converted to Judaism never existed! The coming of the Rus, or the modern name the Russians, was the beginning of the end for the Khazar Kingdom. They were defeated by the Russians in the late 10th century A.D. and by the middle of the 13th century the conquest was complete! This is the point in history where this Kingdom of converted white Jews became lost in history, but how? You can still find their name on ancient maps and the exact location of their kingdom. How could a nation that held off the feared Vikings and the Arabs of Arabia seemingly become lost in the annals of world history? It is simple, upon being defeated by the Russians the Khazar people became incorporated into the rising Russian empire! Note , a large part of the Khazar Jews were concentrated in, Hungary, Crimea, Ukraine, Poland, Lithuanian , Galician , Romania and other states who in turn were conquered and incorporated into the Russian empire. For a reference, see the Palestine plot author B. Jensen pages 2 and 3. The Karites of Poland and Russia are steadfast in that we are the descendants of the Khazar people in this generation! When these people showed up at the United Nations they had no artifacts, and do you know why? Remember these people had there origination in Asia not Mesopotamia and eventually migrated to Europe. The Tarim mummies prove this, the D.N.A, from the 5000 teeth analzed prove this. We know that Jacob had a twin by the name Esau, you know him as Edom, the white Jew looks nothing like Jacob or Esau. See pictures on next page: Ancient Israelite, Aristobulus the Edomite and the unknown white Jew.

ANCIENT (JACOB) ISRAELITES   JOSEPH

ARISTOBULUS ESAU   SALOME ESAU

HERODS GRANDSON   HERODS GRANDAUGHTER

UNKNOWN WHITE JEW

The answer to the white Jewish question is simple, he is not of the seed of Shem based on the statement of King Joseph of Khazaria. He is of Togarmah the son of Japhet the gentile! The historians trace his orgins to Asia and from Asia he ascended into Europe, and his resting place is not in Jerusalem but in the region of the Black Sea and the Caspian Sea. For the sake of argument, I took the images from the tomb of Ben Hassan, the coin with Joseph's image from a museum in Egypt, an image of Herod the Edomites' grandson Aristobulus of Chalcis and his wife Salome and compared them with the European Jew of unknown orgin and the fact of the matter is simple, the white guy does not look like the Edomite (Herod's grandson) money or the images in that region ofthe world! The coin with Aristobulus of Chalcis was used for another reason, it has been stated by brothers of which I hold in high esteem that these white Jews in Jerusalm are Edomites, but if you take a real close look at the coin of Aristobulus he has a big Negro nose, an afro, and the biggest lips I've ever seen. A close examination of Salome's (Herods grandaughter) portrait offers the same clues this woman has braids and Negro features. The money is the secret to the true history of this world and this is something that the coin dealers have known for quite some time. These guys that buy ancient coins buy the true history of the nations.The Herodian line is the line of which brother Aristobulus descended from. This was Esau, Jacobs twin brother. See Genesis 25:20,21, verse 21 and Isaac intreated the Lord for his wife because she was barren and the Lord was intreated of him and Rebekah his wife conceived verse 22 and the children struggled together within her and she said if it be so why am I thus and she went to enquire of the Lord. Verse 23 and the Lord said unto her two nations are in thy womb and two manner of people shall be seperated from thy bowels verse 24 **their were twins in her womb! Verse 25 the elder was called Esau** verse 26 the younger was called Jacob. Per the writings of **Flavious Josephus** we find that this **Herod the Great was a descendant of Esau** who was also called an Edom or Mt Seir or Idumea.

SEED OF ESAU   **SEED OF JACOB**

ARISTOBULUS   **BLACK HEBREW ISRAELITES**

THE TWO SONS OF ISAAC, ESAU AND JACOB, STILL LOOK ALIKE IN THAT THEY ARE PEOPLE OF COLOR!

The European Jews that are currently in Israel look nothing like Herod's grandson Aristobulus, so it is of a certainty that the people in the land are neither Esaus' seed, **Edom,**

ARISTOBULUS THE BLACK EDOMITE:

JACOB THE BLACK HEBREW ISRAELITE: BOTTOM

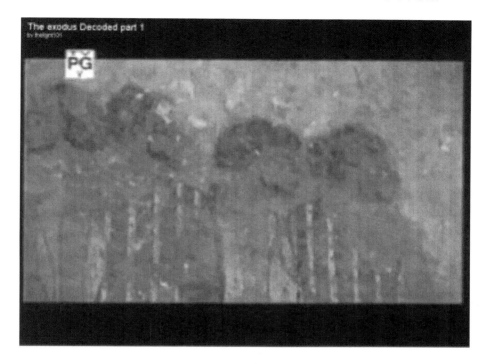

The Edomite Aristobulus, looks just like the black Israelites in the image, It is interesting the value humans place on money, the people who will attempt to hide the truth will burn down libraries and important documents but they never burn the money. Now one might say I'm advocating the theory that the Edomite or Idumea is not in the land. To the contrary, history records that the Jews revolted against the Roman empire in 70 A.D under Vespisian and Titus Caesar. I found a coin that Vespasian had minted to commemerate his defeat of Judah. See the image below.

the inscription on the coin reads, " captive judah, at its present size This coin simply strikes you as another ancient coin. This coin represents the prophecy that Jesus uttered in Luke that Judah would have a trench placed around her and be carried away captive among the gentiles. It also gives credence to the writings of one maligned Jewish historian Flavious Josephus who gave an account of the Roman seige of Jerusalem and wrote that this Vespasian was the Caesar at that time. So this coin is an historical artifact, it depicts a time and place in human history. Indulge me for a moment and look at the page135 as I've enlarged the reverse side of the coin showing the Hebrew captives, the man has an afro and a huge Negroid nose, I had to enlarge this coin to the pages height and width to give you a better understanding of what we are looking at. The man has an afro and a very large Negroid nose and as you know these are not the features of a white male. White males in all of their images depict themselves with straight pointed noses and straight stringy hair. Remember what I told you in previous chapters, the one thing that the Europeans love the most is there money. They will destroy libraries, historical documents, pictures, nations and peoples but never the money. This is their achilles heel , this is the one reason we have uncovered so much truth about the past. The truth about history has been recorded on the money of the past and that is deep to me! **This is the secret of the coin collector.** See the image of the coind **(ancient money)** that I had enlarged on the next page.

Between the years 132-135 A.D and subsequentily were crushed by Hadrian Caesar, after the Romans put down the revolt the Jews were forbidden to enter Jerusalem and it has been recorded that an alien people were permitted to reside in the land of Judah. The next thing that this Hadrian did was **merge** the lands of **Edom, Gailalee, Samaria, Judah** and called it **Palestine**. This brought to pass that passage of scripture in the 83rd psalm verse 4 they have said come and let us cut them off from being a nation that the name of Israel may be no more in remembrance verse 6 **Edom , the Ishmalites (Arabs) Moab**, verse 12 who said let us take to ourselves the houses of God in possession. As these nations did after Nebuchadnezzar destroyed the temple in 587 B.C so these same nations did after the destruction of Jerusalem by Hadrina in 132 A.D, the alien nations the historians are referring to are **Edom, Arabs, Moabites** and so forth. For the sake of visual imagery, I've attached a map for you to see the location of the nations that once surrounded Judah, Ammon, Moab, Arabu(Arabs) and Edom. You can see with the close proximity to Judah the ease with which these nations could ascend and descend into Judah. See map and people of Edom on next page.

THE KINGDOM OF EDOM

ARISTOBULUS THE EDOMITE   SALOME THE EDOMITE

THESE ARE THE PEOPLE OF EDOM: JACOBS TWIN

I've also placed a coin with the images of descendants of the Kingdom of Edom, page 137,this is what the people of Edom looked like, this is Jacobs twin. These images on these coins are undisputed among the archaeologists and by the historians. I've blown up the image of Aristobulus the Edomite on page 139, as large as possible. Make no mistake about it, the lips, hair nose , braids, this is a black Edomite, Jacobs twin! Also see the image of Salome Herod on page 140 she has braids, big lips and a large Negro nose. I present this in my argument as evidence that the people in the land calling themselves Israel or Esau are probably Japhet, straight out of Europe. The book of Obadiah states that when Nebuchadnezzar invaded Judah and carried the population captive that the children of Edom entered the land, Obadiah 1:10-13 verse 13 reads you should not have entered into the gate of my people in the day of their calamity, nor laid hands on their substance. The prophet Ezekiel writes practically the same thing, read the 35th chapter of Ezekiel. Finally the identity theft is recorded in the Illustrated Bible Dictionary, part 1 page 411 and part 2 pages , 825 and 826.

ARISTOBULUS THE EDOMITE: JACOBS TWIN UNDISPUTED BY THE HISTORIANS

NOTICE THE AFRO, BRAIDS NOSE AND LIPS!

IMAGE OF SALOME HEROD: UNDISPUTED!

NOTICE THE BRAIDS, THE LIPS AND THE NOSE

Make no mistake about it this woman has Negroid features! I had to resort to the use of coins to support most of my work because those in the know, who don't want you to know, have burned down the libraries (Julius Caesar burnt the library at Alexandria) broken the nose on the statues of the black Pharaohs (Arabs destroyed black statues of the Pharaohs). In fact Napoleon shot the nose off the Spinx. It has been written of King Leopold of Belgium that for 7 days he was in the Congo destroying government documents. The people who would change history with their lies will go to great lengths to hide the truth. This Aristobulus definitely has an afro, a large Negroid nose and huge lips, not to mention the braids. They have a saying in the streets that even Ray Charles can see this. Before I leave this section I must note the obvious, that based on the physical characteristics of Herods grandchildren one could conclude **that Herod, Philip, Herodias, and Salome of Chalcis** were all black people. In fact the wife of Herod was a **black Maccabean Princess by the name of Miriamne**. This is not conjecture ladies and gentleman this is a historical known fact! Unfortunately there aren't any images to produce of this black princess but go back to the chapter where I deal with the color of Israel according to the scriptures and archaeological evidence, Miriamne was a descendant of Judah, she was black. I must note that it took me two days of research to try to find additonal images of Herod and his offspring but it was fruitless. Most of the coins that had images of his children were so marred that you couldn't distinguish their physical characteristics, the only one worth showing was Aristobulus and his wife Salomne. The one thing that continues to astound me is the D.N.A treasure trove in the land of Israel, it has been noted by the esteemed scientists of this generation that the D.N.A safe box is the teeth. I heard one scientist state that people can write anything in a book suggesting their orgins but the D.N.A dosen't lie it will tell the true tale. To answer the European Jewish question once and for all lets send a team of scientists to the graveyards of Israel and examine the D.N.A of the ancient Israelites and however the pendelum swings so be it! I am also confident that Esau is in the land. Based on the historical evidence it has been surmised that he has mingled himself among the Palestinians and is calling himself a black Palestinian Arab. That is the end of the matter concerning the Negro Question, it is obvious based on the information that I have given in this book that the Negro in America is the Jew of the Bible and antiquity. Now I shall proceed to the last pages of this book by revealing the European secret.

CHAPTER 13   THE EUROPEAN SECRET!

What is this great secret that the Europeans possess that has been omitted from their history books and that would revolutionize the way the world perceives the so called Negro? What if I told you that the so called Negro were the first Kings of Europe? The Roman empire had the distinction of being a multiracial empire. This has been lost on history by the racist reporting by the Europeans in the west, and I shall illustrate this point in a moment. Below is an image of Trajans column and it clearly shows a group of black men with dreadlocks fighting in the Roman army. See blown up version on next page.

Detail from Trajan's Column - Black cavalrymen, allies of the Romans, probably local: absolutely no evidence that they are troops from Africa. The Dacian Wars (101-102, 105-106 A.D.) were two military campaigns fought between the Roman Empire and Dacia during Emperor Trajan's rule. Dacia corresponds to modern countries of Romania and Moldova, as well as smaller parts of Bulgaria, Serbia, Hungary, and Ukraine.

TRAJANS COLUMN: BLACK SOLDIERS DREADLOCKED

Detail from Trajan's Column - Black cavalrymen, allies of the Romans, probably local: absolutely no evidence that they are troops from Africa. The Dacian Wars (101-102, 105-106 A.D.) were two military campaigns fought between the Roman Empire and Dacia during Emperor Trajan's rule. Dacia corresponds to modern countries of Romania and Moldova, as well as smaller parts of Bulgaria, Serbia, Hungary, and Ukraine.

The dread locks can be clearly seen in this ancient snapshot, and the hypothesis is that these brothers were probably part of a contingent from Bulgaria , Serbia, Hungary and the Ukraine. You say this is preposterus, right? Well take a stroll with me thru the Scriputures to a testimony by Paul the Apostle, see Acts 22: verse 24,25,26 and as they bound him with thongs, Paul said unto the centurion that stood by , is it lawful for you to scourge a man that is a Roman and uncondemned? Verse 26 When the centurion heard that he went and told the chief captain saying take heed what thou doest for this man is a Roman. Verse 27 then the chief captain came and said unto him tell me are you a Roman? And Paul said yes. Verse 28 Paul said I was free born! This is the same Paul who was mistaken for an Egyptian and the word Egypt means black. So, we see here that the Apostle Paul was a black Benjamite Roman citizen, but lets examine the 2nd chapter of Acts for there you will see other black Jews come down from Rome on the day of Pentecost. See Acts 2: verse 5 and there were dwelling at Jerusalem Jews devout men out of every nation under heaven. Verse 10 Phrygia and Pamphylia in Egypt and in parts of Libya about Cyrene and **strangers of Rome, Jews** and Proselytes. Did you see that the Roman Empire consisted of black Roman citizens just like you have black American citizens, the Roman empire had black Jews, Edomites (Herodians) black Arabs, Europeans and this is the reason you see dreadlock brothers fighting in Trajans army. Examine this image of the first black Roman Emperor by the name of Septimus Severus born in Libya or Africa , and became Consul in 190 A.D.

SEPTIMUS SEVERUS ROMAN EMPEROR

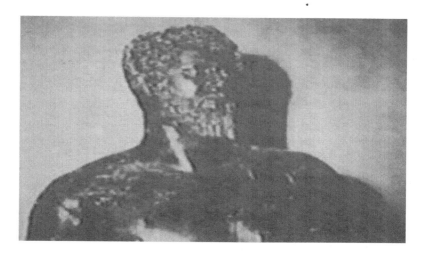

190 A.D

ROMAN EMPEROR PESCENNIUS NIGER 193 A.D

Dosen't his last name ring a bell for all of you Bible geeks? See Acts 13: verse 1 Now there were in the church that was at Antioch certain prophets and teachers as Barnabas and **Simeon that was called Niger!** He was called **Niger because he was black** and for the same reason the black Jew (so called Negro) in America is called Nig#er. No this is not a typing error, I did that on purpose so as not to spell the N word! You will not be able to find the Portugese word Negro on the world maps but you will be able to find the word Niger or Nigeria. This is the region of the world that the Negro in America was stolen from. So the word Nigg## is a misnomer, the true spelling of the word should be Niger. This is a word that denotes where the Negro in America came from. The next image you should be looking at is a German Tapestery found in Germany depicting a black German King being attacked by White barbarians. See the image on the next page.

GERMAN TAPESTERY WILD MEN AND MOORS

1400 A.D

Take a close look at the picture, the black king of Germany and his queen are in the castle while their black subjects fight off the barbarian white Germans. Of particular interest also is that the black warriors have on shoes and are riding horses while the barbarians are barefooted, these are the images that are emerging from Europe.

The next image you should be seeing should probably make you fall out of your seat if you learned history in the west, this image is of a black Otto The Great, the Emperor of the Holy Roman Empire and his black wife, Edith of England, the royalty of England was originally black!

Edith of England and Otto I, Holy Roman Emperor - Married in 929 A.D.

ALESSANDRO DE MEDICI DUKE OF FLORENCE

Alessandro de' Medici (1510-1537), Duke of Penne and also Duke of Florence ruler of Florence from 1530 until 1537.

This is an image of Alessandro De Medici Duke of Florence, a black Duke of Florence but I had never heard of this guy nor seen his image in highschool, college or graduate school Even Stevie Wonder can see this guy is black!

THE BLACK COATS OF ARMS OF EUROPE

Family Crest of: Bower, Bowman, Chatfield, Coults, Fiton, Leader, Miken
(Fairbairn Book of Crests - plate 125)

GERMAN   **BOWER**

This first crest that you are viewing was found in Austria Bavaria, as you can see the image portrays a black man with a bow and arrow. In fact, the Scottish name bower was considered the name of an individual or family of bow makers

GERMAN COAT OF ARMS

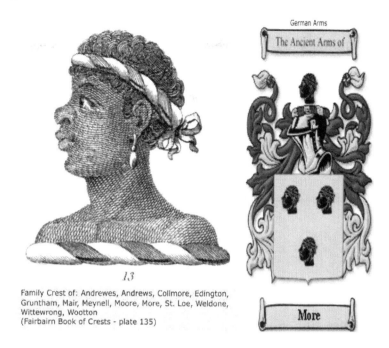

Family Crest of: Andrewes, Andrews, Collmore, Edington, Gruntham, Mair, Meynell, Moore, More, St. Loe, Weldone, Wittewrong, Wootton
(Fairbairn Book of Crests - plate 135)

GERMAN **MOORE**

This black coat of arms was initially found in the Austria. This black coat of arms hence is a relic of the Austrian Empire and again, we find among the German speaking peoples the presence of black nobility.

FRENCH COAT OF ARMS

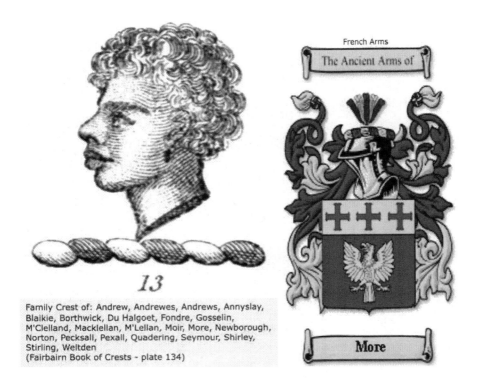

Family Crest of: Andrew, Andrewes, Andrews, Annyslay, Blaikie, Borthwick, Du Halgoet, Fondre, Gosselin, M'Clelland, Macklellan, M'Lellan, Moir, More, Newborough, Norton, Pecksall, Pexall, Quadering, Seymour, Shirley, Stirling, Weltden
(Fairbairn Book of Crests - plate 134)

French **MORE**

This crest was found in France and upon further research, it has been determined that the black family who owned this crest had a place of honor from ancient times.

SCOTTISH COATS OF ARMS

Andros Family Crest
(Entry from Fairbairn's Book of Crests, 1905 ed.)

SCOTLAND   **ANDROS**

This black coat of arms as you probably know was found in Scotland Europe, the story that these images tell is simple, the Negro had power in Mesopotamia, Africa and in Europe. In fact the black man obtained power where ever the sole of his foot tread upon. Andrew, Chief of the clan, rendered homage to King Edward I of England in 1296.

SPANISH COATS OF ARMS

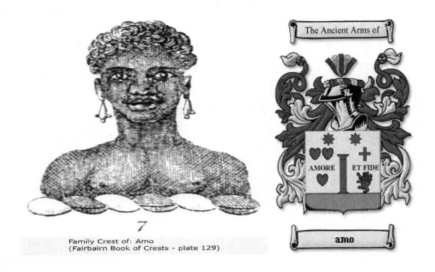

Family Crest of: Amo
(Fairbairn Book of Crests - plate 129)

SPANISH **AMO**

This black coat of arms was found in Spain, this the historians cannot deny. For it is still fresh in the minds of the European historian, concerning the black Moors who ruled Spain. How did all of these black men and women get to Europe before the slave trade? These uninformed generations of historian's seem to conveniently forget one historical fact, and that fact is the Romans were a multiracial Empire. They ruled the known world, white black, red, and orange, it didn't matter to them. Within the empire there were black Kings as long as they paid homage to the Romans. Another fact missed by the historians of this generation, is that Roman Britain was inhabited by Roman citizens before the Jutes,

Angles and Saxons invaded the country by ship. The inhabitants of Roman Britain were a mixture of freed men and women some black and some white. **In the Roman Empire all whites were not free men as one would suppose**. My mind goes back to the Apostle Paul's conversation with the Roman Centurion in Acts the 22nd chapter verse 27,28. Verse 27 reads then the chief captain came and said unto him, tell me, art thou a Roman? He said yea. Verse 28 and the chief captain answered, with a great sum obtained I this freedom. And Paul said, but I was free born, this is the same Paul the Centurion in previous chapters mistook for an Egyptian (Egypt means black). Here is the testimony of a black Jew born as a free Roman citizen. This is the problem that I have with this modern historian, either his vision is blurred or he has no interest in the truth. This modern historian makes the boast that he has attended and graduated from some of the most prestigious Universities in America, but the history that they report is amateurish and unfounded! Now I would be lying if I tried to tell you that black people ruled all of Europe because I can't produce the evidence to substantiate that claim. But I can tell you this with great clarity, this negative image of the Negro as a slave and a servant is an **invention of the United States** and it is not the true image of the so called Negro.

POPE BENEDICT WITH HIS BLACK COAT OF ARMS!

I knew that I would have to show you something shocking to make you see the light, so I present to you the current Pope **Benedict with his black German coat of arms.** The coat of arms to the left of the Pope is the same coat of arms in his background. **This is the coat of arms that this current Pope wears and it is indisputable evidence of the former status of black people in Europe!**

CONCLUSION:

I thought within myself wow, how do you end a book with all of the information that was given to the reader? What could I say that would equal the sensation of the books contents? The first thought that came to my mind was the wisdom of God, how he hid the **truth in the Tombs of the Pharaoh's, on the faces of ancient coins, on statues, on coats of arms, in the historical records of nations themselves, but mostly how God preserved 6000 years of human history in the greatest history book of them all, the Holy Scriptures!** What have I actually done in writing this book? Have I come up with new knowledge, has some new wisdom crept into my mind not so, the only thing that I have done, is what our fathers instructed each and every one of us to do and that is to question all things. People give credit to the Greek philosopher Socrates when they quote the phrase", **man know thyself"**, I am of the opinion that this is God's statement to the inhabitants of the earth, to all nations, peoples, black, white, red, yellow whatever the color of your skin, wake up from your mental slumber and remember who you are. Take the time out of your busy lives and check the record of the past. Examine what occurred before you because as the wise King Solomon said" who can see what will come after him". In 1929 the Vatican question was answered with the passing of the Lateran treaty creating Vatican City and giving complete sovereignty to the Papacy. In 1948 the Jewish question was answered when the United Nations gave the European Jews the land of Judah. The Iraqi question was answered with the assassination of Saddam Hussein and his son's, the Libyan question was answered with the invasion of Libya. The Sudan question was answered with the country being split into two countries, but the Negro question has never been answered. One of the reasons the Negro question has not been answered, is because the artifacts and images have been purposely withheld from the Negro community or whitewashed. The second reason the Negro question went unanswered is because we allowed our enemies to teach us world history, but the history we were taught was white world. Unto this very day our sons and daughters are being taught an erroneous education handed down by the system. The time of our departure is at hand, the King of the universe is on his way back to set the earth back in order. The time that the Most High has set for the ruler ship of the Gentiles has come to an end. The liberation of the son's of God and the poor of this planet is upon us all, God bless you and make sure you recommend this book to someone else, Peace!

GENERAL BIBLIOGRAPHY

JOSEPH J. WILLIAMS, S.J.   HEBREWISMS OF WEST AFRICA, ASHANTI PRIEST CROSSING PRA PG, 83

ARTHUR KOESTLER   THE THIRTEENTH TRIBE EUROPEAN JEWS SONS OF JAPHETH PG, 72 ILLUSTRATED BIBLE DICT   EDOM SEIZES JUDAH PART-1 PG, 411, PART 2- PG, 825,826

KING JAMES   THE BIBLE

SAMUEL KRAMER   THE TABLETS OF SUMER THE BLACK HEADED PEOPLE PGS, 67,123,177

MERRILL C TENNEY   ZONDERVAN PICTORIAL DICT HAM NOT THE PROGENITOR OF THE NEGRO PG, 330

DR. JOSEPH P HOLLOWAY   BLACK HERITAGE 250 BANTU NAMES FOUND IN THE SOUTH PG, 107

YUVAL TAYLOR   FREDERICK DOUGLASS

FREDERICK DOUGLAS DELEGATION PG, 484,486,587

FINAL CALL   WILLIE LYNCH LETTERS

HISTORY CHANNEL   BLACK HEBREW IMAGES

ROBERT MORGAN   INSTITUTE FOR HISTORICAL REVIEW
REVIEW

B JENSEN   PALESTINE PLOT

KHAZARS PG,2

IMAGES TAKEN FROM *WIKIPEDIA ENCYCLOPEDIA*:

SARGON THE GREAT

ELAMITE WARRIOR

IRAQI CITIZENS

KING SHULGI

KING GUDEA

KING SARGON

QUEEN NEFETERI

KING TUT

MODERN EGYPTIANS

KING PREMPEH 1

YAA ASANTE

SLAVE SHIP

NEGRO MALE AND FEMALE FOR SALE SIGN

L OVERTURE TOUSSAINT

NAT TURNER AND NEWS ARTICLE

HARRIET TUBMAN

SOJOURNER TRUTH

IMAGES TAKEN FROM

WIKIPEDIA ENCYCLOPEDIA CONTINUED:

POPE NICHOLAS V

POPE ALEXANDER V1

EMANCIPATION PROCLAMATION

FREDERICK DOUGLAS

FREED SLAVES IN COTTON FIELD

HANGING OF A BLACK MAN

COLORED ONLY RESTAURANTS

MARTIN AND MALCOM

MALCOLMS FUNERAL

MEDGAR EDGARS

JESSEE JACKSON

NUCLEAR BLAST

VAPORIZED HUMANS

HIROSHIMA NUCLEAR IMAGE

DESTROYED CITIES COLOGNE HAMBURG GERM

MASS GRAVES

EUROPEAN JEW

BETA ISRAEL

LEMBA JEWS

MAP IMAGES TAKEN FROM

WIKIPEDIA ENCYCLOPEDIA:

MAP STRABO A.D 15

MAP HERODUTUS 450 B.C

MAP LOCATION OF JEWISH COLONIES

MAP ASHANTI EMPIRE

MAP SLAVE TRADE ROUTE

MAP GOLD COAST SLAVE COAST WHEAT COAST

MAP BIGHT OF BENIN.

MAP OF THE LAND OF THE KHAZARS

COINS & PAPER MONEY IMAGES:

COIN ARISTOBULUS HEROD

WIKIPEDIA ENCYCLOPEDIA.

COIN SALOME HEROD
WIKIPEDIA ENCYCLOPEDIA.

COIN CAPITA JUDEA
WIKIPEDIA ENCYCLOPEDIA.

PAPER MONEY NEGRO CAPTIVE COTTON
WIKIPEDIA ENCYCLOPEDIA.

COIN OF JOSEPH
ARTICLE AL AHRAM NEWS
CAIRO EGYPT.

COIN   HANNABAL OF CARTHAGE

RETAKE YOUR FAME.COM

COIN   BLACK CAESAR NIGER PISCENNIUS

ARTICLE: AFRICANS WHO CONQUERED ROME

JIDE UWECHIA, AUTHOR.

BLACK JESUS - COPTIC MUSEUM CAIRO EGYPT

JUDGEMENT SCENE- MAVRIOTISSA MONASTERY

- NORTHERN GREECE

IMAGES FROM NEWS MATTERS PUBLICATIONS:

POPE BENEDICT PRAYING TO BLACK JESUS

POPE JOHN PAUL 2 PRAYING TO BLACK JESUS

MEXICO BLACK JESUS

FRANCE BLACK JESUS

BRAZIL BLACK JESUS

SPAIN BLACK JESUS

ARK OF COVENANT   PROF TUDOR PARFITT

UNIVERSITY OF LONDON

HAGAB JUDEAN ARCHER   FERRELL JENKINS

AFRICANS WHO CONQUERED ROME ARTICLE

BY JIDE UWECHIA, AUTHOR:

TRAJANS COLUMN   BLACK ROMANS DREADLOCKS

NIGER PISCENNIUS BLACK ROMAN CAESAR

SEPTIMUS SEVERUS BLACK ROMAN CAESAR.

PERSIAN GUARDS- WIKIPEDIA ENCYCLOPEDIA

XERXES THE PRINCE- WIKIPEDIA ENCYCLOPEDIA

GERMAN TAPESTRY   MOORISH HISTORY

DAISHIKI JONES.

OTTO THE GREAT   ANCIENT MAN & HIS FIRST CIVILIZATIONS.

COATS OF ARMS   FAIRBAIRN BOOK OF CRESTS: THE FAMILIES OF GREAT BRITAIN AND IRELAND

PAINTING SCENE MARI   BLACK SUMERIANS
KEMET WAY.COM
EMAIL ADDRESS: lee0260@comcast.net

BLACK MESOPOTAMIANS

The Treasury at Persepolis (Parsa): Persian guards

BLACK MESOPOTAMIAN KING

Prince Xerxes behind the throne of King Darius

The Negro Act!!

Repeat after me! I am obligated after reading this book to tell somebody in my church, grammar school, highschool or college about it. I am obligated to give this book to my pastor and my deacons, I am obligated to have this book sitting in my house on the coffee table with my bible for it is a treasure within itself. This is the thing that the Europeans fear the most and that is the reverse brainwashing of the Negro in America.

Jesus said" You shall know the truth and the truth shall set you free".

GO IN PEACE FOR YOU ARE FREE!!

Made in the USA
San Bernardino, CA
11 November 2016